CW00644324

More Grain *for the* Famine

by James Jacob Prasch

Published by
SMP Ltd
1 Barnfield, Common Lane, Hemingford Abbots
Cambridgeshire PE28 9AX UK
Tel: +(0)1480 399098
Email: *PF.SMP@dial.pipex.com*

ISBN 1-9015460-7-1

All scripture quotes taken from the New American Standard Bible
© The Lockman Foundation 1960, 1962, 1963, 1968, 1971, 1972, 1973,
unless otherwise noted.

First Edition 2002
© Copyright. James Jacob Prasch 2000,2001,2002

Printed in the UK

CONTENTS

Foreword

IN this present environment the Christian is faced with all manner of opinions, thoughts, testimonies and pseudo doctrines. Many churches and individuals are submitting themselves to the ecumenical idealistic ways of mankind instead of to the total will of God; consequently many books written and many messages given under the umbrella of Christian teaching, are little more than the corrupt ideas of fallen man.

It is such a blessing and often a challenge to the Christian when someone comes with a book or a teaching that is biblically based. This book and the teaching herein bring such a blessing and such a challenge. The topics covered in this book are topics every Christian needs to understand, especially at this present time.

Jacob Prasch is a preacher who brings strong biblically-based teaching to the "church". It is my belief that our Lord and saviour, through His grace and mercy, has given Jacob a gift to open and expand the scriptures allowing many Christians, such as myself and countless others, to grow in our understanding of God's precious word.

His messages, whether written or oral, contain strong meat for the Christian to digest. Sadly he has suffered much personal criticism because he will not bend over backwards and compromise the word of God, but prefers to bend forward in prayer seeking the will of God. His balanced exegesis of God's word is so refreshing and much can be learned from the teachings of my Christian brother and friend Jacob Prasch.

I encourage you to take the time to read this book and if at times you find within the pages, areas that challenge your thoughts, please be as a Berean and test what is written with scripture.

In His service,

Philip Hammond

Midrash: Jesus in the Garden

S OME of you may not be familiar with Moriel Ministries, so I will take a few minutes to explain one of the things that we do. We try to help Christians to understand the Bible in its original context of the first-century church, which was established by the Lord through Jewish Christians. We try to read the Bible the same way the early Jewish church would have read it. There have been others who have tried to do that through the centuries, with varying degrees of success — most notably the Plymouth Brethren. We believe it to be important in the Last Days to understand how to interpret the Bible in the way the first-century church did.

(For those who already know this, I apologise. However, there may be readers who are new to our teaching or who are new in the faith, and for their sakes all of this bears repeating.)

When a Jewish Christian in the first century read the first four chapters of John's gospel, he would have said that it parallels the book of Genesis. He would have said that the story of the new creation in John's gospel is a midrash on, or an inquiry into, the creation. The new creation in John corresponds to the creation in Genesis. Genesis tells us that God walked the earth, and Adam heard Him in the garden of Eden. This speaks of Jesus: it is a Christophany, which is the theological term for an Old Testament manifestation of Jesus. John tells us in his first chapter that His Word became flesh, and once again God walked the earth.

The creation account in Genesis speaks of the small light and the great light, referring to the moon and the sun. In John, we again find the small light—John the Baptist, whose Hebrew name is *Yochanon Ha Matbil*—and the great light—Jesus the Messiah, whose Hebrew name is *Yeshua Ha Mochiach*.

In Genesis, God's Spirit moved on the water and brought forth the creation. In John chapter four we hear of those who are born of water and of the Spirit. Again, the Spirit moved on the water, this time to bring forth the new creation. On the third day of creation in Genesis, God does a miracle with water. In John 2:1, we read that the wedding at Cana is on the third day, and once more God does a miracle on the third day with water—this time in the new creation. God began His first plan for man with the marital union of Adam and Eve; Jesus began His public ministry at a wedding in Cana, and God's second plan for man also commences with a marital union. The new creation in John is full of parallels with the creation in Genesis; one is a midrash of the other.

There are many things in scripture that are like this. The Tree of Life in Judaism, which in Hebrew is called the *es hayyim*, is represented by a fig tree. We see it in Ezekiel 47 and also in the book of Revelation, but we see it first in the creation account in Genesis. In John chapter one, when Nathaniel asks Jesus how He knows so much about him, Jesus answers, *"Because I saw you under the fig tree."* What Jesus was saying to Nathaniel with these words was not simply that he saw him under a literal fig tree, (although that was a part of it), what He was really saying in midrash, or Jewish metaphor, is this: "I saw you from the garden, from the creation, from the foundation of the world".

Genesis and John—creation and new creation. Compare the Bible to a loaf of bread straight out of the baker's oven: before it has been sliced, it looks the same on both ends. In the same way, scripture tells us that the Lord declares the end from the beginning. If we cut this loaf open, we arrive at John's gospel. Most conservative evangelicals believe that the same John who wrote the gospel also wrote the book of Revelation. In light of this, we see that we have first the creation, next the new creation, but then also the re-creation. If you look at Genesis in comparison with Revelation, you will see this kind of parallel. Once more in Revelation we see the Tree of Life that we first saw in Genesis. In Genesis 49 we find Jacob's prophecy to the twelve tribes of Israel; lo and behold, in Revelation seven and fourteen we find the twelve tribes once more.

Revelation tells us that *"The dragon and the serpent are cast down to you"*. I don't believe that the dinosaurs are billions of years old, as stated in that interpretation known as the gap theory. The serpent was once quadrupedal or bipedal; in other words, it walked.

It is interesting to note that every civilization from Mexico to China has stories of dragons. I've been a number of times to the Taronga Zoo in Sydney, Australia, and what a fantastic zoo it is! What would you call a lizard that measures nine or ten feet long by three feet high by two to three feet wide, and that could eat you? We call it a Komodo dragon. The word 'dinosaur' means simply 'great and terrible lizard'; I have seen them alive in our time.

To return to our point, the *dragon* spoken of in Revelation is Satan the persecutor; the serpent is Satan the deceiver. Jesus said in Matthew 23 that Abel was the first martyr: *"Your brother's blood cries out"*, God tells Cain in Genesis. What do we see in Revelation? That the blood of the martyrs under the altar is crying out.

Then in Genesis we are told of Joseph's vision of the woman with the stars. In Revelation, there again, is the woman with the stars, in chapter 12. The parallels go on and on and on like that. Again, the Bible is like a loaf of bread; it looks the same from both ends before you cut it. When you do cut it, you see the pattern: creation, new creation, and re-creation.

With this background in view, turn with me, please, to the book of Genesis chapter three. In Hebrew we call Genesis *Bereshit*, meaning 'In the Beginning'. Verse 5:

> "'For God knows,' said the serpent, 'that in the day you eat from it, your eyes will be opened and you will be like God, knowing good and evil.' When the woman saw that the tree was good for food and it was a delight to the eyes, and the tree was desirable to make one wise, she took from its fruit and ate, and she gave also to her husband with her, and he ate."

We see here the lust of the eyes, the lust of the flesh and the boastful pride of life of which we are warned in John's epistle. John, author of the Revelation and of the gospel of John, is also the author of three epistles. We find midrashes on Genesis throughout his work; the lust of the eyes, the lust of the flesh, and the boastful pride of life is yet another example.

Generically, in God's economy there are only two men: the first Adam and the last Adam. When you were physically born, you were born of Adam. When you are born again, you are born of the last Adam, who is Jesus.

The second Adam, Jesus, had to be like Adam in certain aspects. Adam and Jesus were both created directly by God without procreative agency (Jesus pre-existed but His body was created), and they were both created without sin. The first Adam, however, fell into sin. Before Jesus could go to the cross and take our sin upon Himself, He had to reverse what the first Adam had done. That is why in Mark chapter one, when it describes the temptation of Jesus, the text says that He was with the wild animals the same way Adam was. The picture of Jesus in the character of Adam is here being painted. Satan then comes to Jesus holding out the same three temptations into which Adam and Eve fell: the lust of the eyes, the lust of the flesh, and the boastful pride of life. What the first Adam fell into, the second Adam did not. Before Jesus could go to the cross, He had to overcome what the first Adam was overcome by. Then and only then could He go to the cross. That is why the text states, *"And Satan departed from Him until the appropriate time"*. At their first encounter, Satan had to try to make Jesus fall into the same sin the first Adam did. At their second, He could and did take our sin. Jesus could not go to the cross on our behalf until He had reversed what the first Adam did; until He overcame where the first Adam failed.

At this point we will take a closer look at the phrase "to know" the Hebrew word 'to know' is *la daot*, and the Greek term is *gnosco*. The serpent was already in the garden when Adam and Eve were told to subdue the earth; they were always meant to know that evil existed, and to know objectively what it was; but they were not to know it within themselves. They were not to know it experientially, although they were to know it existed. We already know that the Tree of Life was present in the Garden of Eden; the Tree of the Knowledge of Good and Evil was also there. Adam and Eve had a choice between those trees: the Tree of Life or the Tree of the Knowledge of Good and Evil. They chose to try to be their own gods, to gain knowledge they were not meant to have. They were to know that evil existed, but they were not to know it within themselves. To understand this, we must grasp the different kinds of knowledge, of which we have two biblical examples.

The first example is found in the high priest on the Day of Atonement: only the high priest could enter the Holy of Holies, and even he only once a year on *Yom Kippur*, the Day of Atonement. Any Hebrew, however, could read the book of Leviticus and know what was inside the Holy of Holies. He could read descriptions of the furniture, the shewbread, the Ark of the Covenant, etc., and in that sense he could know what was in there. Only the high priest, however, could know what it was like to go in there, because he was designated for it. He was sanctified, or set apart, for that purpose: in Hebrew that is, *me kudesh*. The Hebrew terms 'to know' and 'to sanctify', as in 'to set apart'—*La daot* and *Le heet kodesh*—frequently go together in the Bible. Anybody could know what was inside the Holy of Holies, but only the person who was sanctified for the purpose was to know what it was like to go into the holy of holies.

The other time that these two terms are used in connection with each other is in holy matrimony. Anybody can get a copy of Gray's Anatomy and look at the female body: one can look at diagrams, charts, and pictures of ovarian tissue, fallopian tubes, uterine tissue, or any other aspect of female anatomy; it is all in the textbooks. Anybody may know what comprises a woman's body. The Hebrew term, however, for "to wed" means 'to make holy, to sanctify'. During a Jewish wedding you say *Me kudesh*, or "with this ring, I wed thee", literally "sanctify"; set apart according to the laws of Moses and Israel. The word for 'to marry' and the word for 'to sanctify' is the same. The Hebrew word for 'to consummate a marriage' is 'to know'.

Anybody can know what is inside a woman's body; but only the man sanctified for the purpose is to know what it is like to go in. In the same way, anybody could know what was inside the Holy of Holies, but no one except the high priest could know what it was like to go in there. It is the same with *gonosko*, the Greek term. Adam and Eve were always meant to know that there was evil, and that there was a devil. They were intended to know that things had to be subdued on the earth, though it was not yet fallen. They were meant to know objectively, but they were not meant to know experientially. They were to know, but they were not to know.

"Then the eyes of both of them opened, and they knew that they were naked, and they sewed fig leaves together and made themselves loin coverings."

Nakedness in the Bible does not simply mean the nudity on beaches in places such as Maui, Hawaii, or Elat, Israel. The new-agers in such places swim naked and have tattoos of dragons, of flowers, or of any number of other things in places you would not think that people would or should have tattoos; they run around on the beach naked, like the heathens they are. That, however, is not what this is primarily talking about. Adam and Eve were literally naked, yes, but it meant something more than that. Remember the church of Laodicea in Revelation: *"You do not know that you are wretched, pitiable, poor, blind and naked"*. As Isaiah said, nakedness symbolises not having the garments of salvation. Adam and Eve knew that now they needed to be saved, for they had sinned.

In their guilt, therefore, they sewed fig leaves together. Remember what we see in Genesis and in Revelation: a fig tree. In Revelation, the text states that the fig leaves are for the healing of the nations; biblically, therefore, fig leaves are figures or symbols of good works.

Adam and Eve sewed fig leaves together, and in the same way, fallen man will always try to justify himself before a sinless God with good works. Every religion on earth is the diametric opposite of the gospel. When God— that is, Jesus—found Adam and Eve in the Garden wearing their fig leaves, He rejected the fig leaves and said that there must be blood atonement in order to remove sin. Religion is man trying to reach God with good works; the gospel is God trying to reach man with blood atonement. Religion is man trying to reach God; the gospel is God trying to reach man. Again, religion is the diametric opposite to the gospel, no matter what form it takes. It makes no difference whether it is the Jehovah's Witnesses and the Mormons knocking on doors, an Orthodox Jew trying to keep the *mitzvot*, a Catholic at the Novena, or a Muslim at the hajj. Every religion is based on sewing fig leaves together in a futile attempt to be justified before God. There is, however, absolutely no assurance of salvation in that. On the contrary, the scriptures tell us directly that *"all of our righteous deeds are as filthy rags"*. Am I saying that Mother Theresa's righteous deeds are filthy rags? No, I am not saying that; God is.

Christians do not do good works in order to get saved; real Christians do good works rather because we have been saved. It is not our righteousness, but the righteousness of Christ in and through us. That is totally different from man-made religion. We do good works because we've been saved, not in an attempt to attain salvation for ourselves. This leads to why Jesus cursed the fig tree: it had leaves, but no fruit; in the same way, Israel had a works righteousness based on legalism, but it did not have the fruit of the Holy Spirit.

We should understand that the leaves are certainly important. In the Middle East, the sun is so hot that without leaves the fruit would be destroyed. On a fig tree in particular, the fruit grows underneath the leaves. When Jesus cursed this tree, however, the text states that it was not yet the season for figs. The warning we must glean from this is that the *"Son of Man comes at an hour you do not expect"*; we must live in readiness at all times. Again, without leaves the fruit would be destroyed; as James tells us, *"Faith without works is dead"*. There's nothing wrong with the leaves, but the fact is that you cannot eat them. Even the best leaves do not make up for a lack of fruit, although you need the leaves. We are not told that we will know people by their works, but that we will know them by their fruit. It should be noted that works can be evidence of fruit, because the leaves normally appear at about the same time as the fruit; but an abundance of leaves is not a guarantee that you will find fruit.

Adam and Eve sewed fig leaves together, just as today every religion still does. There are many non-evangelical 'churches' that think they are Christian. If you ask them, "How do you get to heaven?", they will tell you that it is accomplished by having enough good deeds to outweigh your bad deeds, or something similar. What do they do to hide their nakedness? They sew fig leaves together. What do they do at the Mass? They sew fig leaves together. What do they do down at the mosque? They sew fig leaves together. Every religion sews fig leaves together, even though it is useless in gaining salvation. For that, there must be a blood atonement.

So the story continues:

> "And they heard the sound of the Lord God walking in the Garden in the cool of the day."

The Hebrew word for 'cool' is also the Hebrew word for 'breeze' or 'wind', *ruach*. The Hebrew word for 'breeze', by turn, is also the Hebrew word for 'spirit': *Pneuma* in Greek, *ruach* in Hebrew. So you have here the presence of the Holy Spirit implied in the Hebrew text.

> "And the man and his wife hid themselves from the presence of the Lord among the trees of the garden. And the Lord called to the man and said to him, 'Where are you?'"

We notice here that it speaks of the 'trees of the garden'; concerning the Last Days, Jesus never said we must learn the parable of the fig tree. When you read it in Luke, He actually said, *"Learn the parable of the fig tree and the other trees,"* or, *"and all the trees"*. This is not our subject today, I merely point it out in passing to say that there is much more to the parable of the fig tree than most Christians have a clue about. In fact, the parable of the fig tree and the other trees is found in the Book of Judges chapter nine. But let us continue.

We see now the cast of characters introduced in the Garden; first and foremost, we have God in the person of Jesus, a Christophany. We have Satan in his mode as a deceiver. Then we have naked man. So far, we have three characters: God, Satan, and a naked man. Let us continue with the text:

> "And he said, 'I heard the sound of the thee in the garden and I was afraid because I was naked, so I hid myself.' And He said, 'Who told you that you were naked? Have you eaten from the Tree of which I commanded you not to eat?'"

This sounds perhaps as if God didn't know; God knew, of course, but He was challenging Adam.

> "And the man said, 'The woman whom Thou gavest to me, she gave me from the Tree and I ate.'"

Notice that although God in His omniscience already knew who ate first, He doesn't go to Eve but to Adam. If something, God forbid, goes wrong in my marriage or my family, or in your marriage or your family, gentlemen, it might not be our fault, but as far as God's concerned, it is our problem; the male is God's authority in that relationship.

In the Bible, every time a man lets a woman take spiritual headship, you have a disaster. Abraham and Sarah or Ahab and Jezebel are two examples of this. This goes right back to the garden of Eden, and as such is one of Satan's oldest tricks. Why is leadership into this error now? We will see that in a moment, but let's continue.

And the man said in verse 12,

> "'The woman whom thou gavest to be with me, she gave me from the Tree and I ate.' Then the Lord God said to the woman, 'What is this you have done?' And the woman said, 'The serpent deceived me and I ate.' And the Lord God said to the serpent, 'Because you have done this, cursed are you more than all the cattle and more than every beast of the field. On your belly you shall go, and dust you shall eat all the days of your life. And I will put enmity between you and the woman, between your seed and her seed. He shall bruise you on the head, and you shall bruise him on the heel'" (because of the resurrection). "To the woman, He said, 'I will greatly multiply your pain in childbirth. You shall bring forth children, yet your desire shall be for your husband and he shall rule over you.' Then God said to Adam, 'Because you have listened to the voice of your wife and have eaten from the Tree about which I commanded you ...'"

Notice the curse is on Satan first, women second, and men third. Satan first, women second, and men third; the judgment was given in the order of the sin.

Because of the Fall, men have become insensitive. Also because of the Fall, women have become hypersensitive. When a husband and wife get saved, most of the time it is the wife who gets saved first. This is not always the case, but probably at least 75 percent of the time the wife gets saved first. If the husband does get saved first, 75 percent of the time the wife eventually gets saved also; water takes the shape of its container. If the wife gets saved first, however, it is usually a much harder situation. Christian women often grieve for years over their unbelieving husbands. Why is it easier for women to get saved? It is because they are more sensitive. When a husband and wife pray together for direction, it is usually the wife who hears from the Lord first and clearest; men are reliant on female sensitivity because of the Fall. On the other hand, while it is usually easier for women to hear the voice of the Holy Spirit, it is also easier for women to hear the voice of a counterfeit spirit and thus fall into deception, to be taken in by spiritual seduction. Women are much more vulnerable to spiritual seduction than are men. Therefore, just as men are reliant on female sensitivity, so women are reliant on male protection. The submission in a Christian marriage is to be mutual, but in different ways; it is an equality with different functions, but the buck stops with the man. Women are more vulnerable to spiritual seduction, while men are more vulnerable to not hearing at all. That's just the way it is in our fallen world. There may have been a propensity towards that before man fell, but the Fall brought it to be what it is now.

It all happens in a garden. Next, God dispatches an angel and says, "Get out of here. You cannot come in anymore." Here we are introduced to the fourth character, the angel who says 'get out'. In this garden, man falls. In this garden, God pronounces a curse on men and on women. In this garden, the angel says 'do not come in here.' In this garden man is naked before his God.

Yet in this garden, there is also a promise of salvation: *"'I will put enmity between you and the woman, between your seed and her seed.'"* As most of you know, Eve represents Israel and by extension the church. The church is the bride of Christ, and Israel is God's woman.

Anti-Semitism and persecution of the believing church are heads and tails; two sides of the same coin. We can distinguish between the two, but we cannot separate them. God's plan for the salvation of the world depends on his prophetic agenda for Israel and the Jews and for the believing church. The two kinds of people whom the Bible calls Abraham's children are the Jews and the believing church. The return of Jesus Christ depends on the prophetic plan of God for Israel and the Jews, and for the believing church. Hence, the Jews and the believing church have the same enemy. Why do you think the Muslims hate Israel and hate America? Is it purely political? No. There is a spiritual reason. At this time in history America is the seat of evangelical Christianity, as Britain was a hundred, two hundred years ago, and as Germany and Switzerland were during the Reformation.

"I'll put enmity between you and the woman, between your seed and her seed." Look at pagan Rome: first, they turned against the church under Nero. A few years later, they turned against the Jews under Titus. A few centuries later, it happened under the communists in the Soviet Union. Who did the Soviets persecute the most? Jews and born-again Christians! Throughout the centuries of the inquisitions, the pogroms, the massacres—who did the Roman Catholic Church persecute the most? Jews and born-again Christians. What do Arafat's followers say?

What don't they show you on CNN? They don't show you that the Islamic Arabs whom they champion are the same people who say every day of the week, "First the Saturday people, then the Sunday people. Jihad! Jihad!" In other words, first we kill the Jews, and then we kill the Christians. I will put enmity between you and the woman, between your seed and her seed.

It all happens in a garden. With this in view, let us look at the midrash: Turn to John chapter 18 verse one:

> "When Jesus had spoken these words, He went forth with His disciples over the ravine of Kidron where there was a garden into which He Himself entered and His disciples."

Of the four gospels, the one that identifies Gethsemane as a garden is John. John, again, is always interested in doing a midrash on Genesis. The Kidron is a narrow valley between the Temple Mount on the west and the Mount of Olives or *Har Zeitim* on the east. Gethsemane comes from the Hebrew word *Shemen*, or 'oil'. The olive oil—which we call *Shemen ziot*—used ritually in the Temple came from Gethsemane. They would harvest the olives growing on the Mount of Olives, and bring them to Gethsemane to be pressed. (There are still olive orchards on the Mount of Olives to this day; in fact, the experts tell us that there are trees there that are 2,000 years old and still growing; they would have been present in the days of Jesus. Olive trees live an extremely long time if they are not interrupted by earthquakes or pollution or other environmental catastrophes). It is to Gethsemane that Jesus goes, and there something begins to happen.

To God, one man without sin is worth more than all the men with sin: that is how one could die for all. In this garden, God takes our sin on Himself. He takes our sin and puts it on His son, Jesus, in order to take His righteousness and put it on us.

Jesus suffered physically; He was tortured. He suffered emotionally; the Bible speaks of this time as the "travail of his soul". But something else happened on the cross: His fellowship was broken with His Father. We must note also that He said, *"It is finished. Father, into your hands I give My Spirit."* Satan's liars in the church today deny this fundamental doctrine: Copeland, Hagen, Joyce Meyer, all these people are teaching error. They teach that Satan got the victory on the cross, that Jesus' Spirit was not commended to the Father, that it was not finished, and that He had to go to Hell. They teach further that He was tortured in Hell for three days and three nights, and that then He had to be born again in Hell. That is the teaching of Copeland and Hagen, which they got from E.W. Kenyon. They have another Jesus; they have another gospel, as most of you know. Because the cross of Jesus is not central to their view of salvation, neither is the cross of Jesus central to their view of the Christian life. Instead of "pick up your cross and follow Me", their doctrine is "you're a King's kid, name it and claim it, God wants you rich, believe God for another Mercedes, etc". These men are from the devil, and are some of the false prophets that Jesus warned would come in the Last Days. Today they are doing exactly what Jesus said they would do.

Jesus takes our sin on Himself, not in Hell, but in a garden. That is where God begins to put our sin on Jesus.

And then, the full wrath of God was poured out on Jesus while He was on the cross.

> "Now, Judas also, who was betraying Him, knew the place, for the disciples had often met there. (Jesus often met there with His disciples) Judas then, having received the Roman cohort and officers from the chief priests and the Pharisees, came there with lanterns and torches and weapons. Jesus, therefore, knowing all the things that were coming upon Him, went forth and said to them, 'Whom do you seek?' And they answered Him, 'Jesus, the Nazarene.'"

Jesus' real name was *Rabbi Yeshu BarYosefvi Netzeret*. They wouldn't have known who Jesus Christ is, but they would have known who Rabbi Yeshua was; He is the one who raises the dead and heals the lepers; He is the one who could walk on water.

> "When, therefore, He said to them, 'I am He', they drew back and fell to the ground."

The Greek text says that they fell back and then they slid forward. Every knee will bow, even those of His enemies.

The phenomenon of being "slain in the spirit" happens at various times in the Bible, particularly in the New Testament. In Revelation chapter one, John is in the Spirit in the Lord's day, and when the power of Jesus comes on him, he falls as if slain. He fell forward, and was so terrified that God had to send an angel to encourage him. When Jesus cast a demon out of the child whom the demons kept throwing into the fire, they thought he was dead; but when he got up he was completely different. Daniel, too, was terrified.

Notice that in the Bible whenever someone was slain in the Spirit it was a once in a lifetime life-changing event. It doesn't matter what happens when people go down, how different is their life once they get up? But today, who is getting in line to be slain? The very same ones who were in line to go down last week. They just want to go down for the thrill of it. As with anything else, a wicked and adulterous generation seeks this sign.

Again, in the Bible being slain in the Spirit was a once in a lifetime, life-changing experience. It doesn't matter what happens when somebody goes down, but how changed their life is when they get up. In the Bible, too, whenever it was a blessing from God, the person in question went forward. The only time they ever went backwards was when it was a curse and a judgment: when they came to arrest Christ.

Today you see Rodney Howard Brown and these guys bringing official 'catchers' with them. But they are falling the wrong direction. People insist that they know this experience is from God; well, it might be indeed, but if it is, He is angry with them. I personally am pretty certain that most of it is hypnotic induction combined with demonic deception. Even if it is of God, however, it is a judgment.

Whom do you seek? Jesus. I am He. In Greek, "I am He," or, *ego eimi*. The Greek equivalent is also found at the end of John chapter 8, where Jesus says, *"before Abraham was, I am." Ego eimi.* The people then tried to stone Him, because He made Himself equal with God.

Let us go back to our cast of characters: In the garden of Eden is God in the Person of Jesus. In the garden of Gethsemane is God in the Person of Jesus. But then, in the garden of Eden, Satan as deceiver is present. In the gospel of John, what happens to Judas just before the disciples accompany Jesus to Gethsemane? The text plainly tells us: Satan entered him. The only two people demon-possessed by Satan personally will be the Antichrist or false prophet, and Judas, the Son of Perdition. John in his epistle describes Antichrist in the character of Judas. *"They went out from among us, but they were not really of us."* Whenever you see something about Judas in the Bible, the Holy Spirit is telling you something about the anti-Christ. Both Judas and the Antichrist will be into money; both can deceive the brethren. The disciples were asking, *"Lord is it I, Lord is it I?"*—they did not know the identity of the traitor until Jesus revealed him. In the same way, people will not know who the real anti-Christ is until Jesus reveals him. If you cannot see through Benny Hinn or Kenneth Copeland or Chuck Colson, what will become of you when the Antichrist comes?

How did Judas con people? He conned people with the Mother Theresa trick: fig leaves. *"Could this not have been sold and given to the poor?"*—he feigned compassion for the poor in order to ingratiate himself with people, to make them think he was a good guy. In reality, however, he was only using the plight of the poor to seduce, camouflage, and manipulate. Mother Theresa said before she died that she had no assurance of salvation. When she got the Nobel Prize, she made it clear that she did not convert people in India to be Christians, but to be better Hindus and better Muslims. That was her gospel. She cleaned them up, gave them a clean place to die with dignity, and sent them off to Hell in the name of the Father, the Son, and the Holy Spirit in a laundry chute.

The Antichrist will do the same thing. He's going to pretend to care for the poor and thus manipulate people into thinking he's a wonderful humanitarian. Notice, too, that if you tell the truth about Mother Theresa, even most Christians will be outraged that you would dare say that about that great "saint of God". You may only be quoting her, but she is beyond reproach in their eyes. The Antichrist is going to make Mother Theresa look like a combination of Jezebel and Ma Barker... terrible, horrible.

In the garden once more, at Gethsemane, we have Satan in his mode as deceiver. Who else is in the garden? Let us look at this in the synoptic gospels very briefly. Turn to Mark 14:51.

> "When they came to arrest Jesus, a certain young man was following Him, wearing nothing but a linen sheet."

Here we have a man who, when they come to arrest Jesus, runs away naked. He is a type of the people who, at the time of persecution, will backslide. They run away without the garment of salvation in an attempt to save their necks. Many will fall away.

The problem with persecution is that it is the ones who do not need the persecution who get it first and worst. The others, however, when it does come, will fall away.

Remember that Jesus said, *"Many will fall away and betray one another."* The Christians who are going to fall away and betray you tomorrow are the ones who listen to Copeland and Hagen today. If someone is being told the lie that God wants you rich, you don't have to suffer, you're a king's kid", only to find themselves suffering, what hope have they of keeping their faith? Their faith, sadly, was never real to begin with. I'm a Pentecostal, but the distortion of Pentecostalism is as apostate as is the Roman Catholic Church, the Greek Orthodox Church, or the liberal Protestants. It's all from the devil. It's all Satan's deception.

To return to our cast of characters, we now have God, we have Satan, and we have the naked man in the garden. *"Whom do you seek? Jesus, the Nazarene." "I am He."* Then we read that it happens again: *"Whom do you seek? Jesus the Nazarene," he replies, "I told you that I am He."* Three times, Jesus says *"I am"*. *"If therefore you seek me, let these go their way"*—this is a corporate solidarity; "corporate solidarity" is the theological term for describing where one person represents a larger group of people. There are many corporate solidarities in John's gospel.

I'll give you two examples of corporate solidarity: *Bar Abbas* in Aramaic means "Son of the Father". He was the equivalent of a modem terrorist. I live in England, and I go to Northern Ireland frequently, where you have the IRA and the UVF; the Protestant and Catholic terrorists. These people are basically gangsters who are perpetrating what amounts to organised crime in the name of a political religious cause. Both the Protestants and the Catholics do it. They are basically gangsters—religious hypocrites of the most atrocious description. That is fairly equivalent to what Barabbas was like.

"Whom shall I give you?" Pilate asks the people. "This terrorist or Rabbi Yeshua?" Do you want this murderer, or do you want this Rabbi who brought the little girl back to life? Who made the blind see, the lame walk, and the deaf hear, who healed the lepers, who taught people about love, peace and truth?

"Give us Barabbas", their demand for Barabbas is a picture of us all: the just for the unjust. Bar Abbas, Son of the Father. We become sons of the Father because Jesus went to the cross in our place. All four gospels put the gospel in the forum of a judicial proceeding—Jesus was put on trial in our place.

John Wimber, however, said, "We're going to take the gospel out of the judicial forum". John Wimber had a message from Hell. All four gospels put the gospel into a judical forum and you cannot know God as loving Father until you know Him as a righteous judge.

Another corporate solidarity is one of the apostles: We have the colloquialism even in English, a 'Doubting Thomas'. He wasn't the only apostle who doubted, but he did, saying *"I won't believe until I see the pierce marks"*. According to Zechariah 12:10, when Jesus comes back, the Jews will *"look upon Him whom they have pierced, and mourn as one mourns for an only son, weeping bitterly over Him like the bitter weeping over a firstborn"*. This is when unbelieving Israel will believe—when they see the pierce-marks. Thomas is a corporate solidarity; he's a picture of his fellow Jews.

There is another corporate solidarity: *"Whom do you seek?"* *"Jesus"* *"I am He. Let these go"*. Who are "these"? Peter, James, and John; who represent you and me.

"Whom do you seek?" "Jesus."

"I am He; let these go."

"Well, what about Jacob Prasch? You know, that guy who worked his way through college selling cocaine?"

"Let him go. I'm the one you're looking for; take me."

"But he was the campus radical who firebombed a police car!"

"Yeah, I know who he was, and I know what he did. I saw him under the fig tree. Let him go."

"Well, what about the homosexual?"

"Let him go. Take me; I'm the one you're looking for."

"What about the pimp?"

"Let him go. I'm the one you're looking for."

"What about the prostitute?"

"Let her go. I'm the one you're looking for, let these go."

"Let them go? They're criminals!"

"I know who they are, but you're looking for me. Let these go. Take me. Let these go."

"Who are you?"

"I am the I Am. This is my game. I'm the one who walks in the garden. I made these rules. We're playing my game, by my rules. Let these go, and take me."

That's the gospel. They did as He said, and let them go. And it happened in a garden. Let us continue looking at the garden:

Turn, please, to chapter John 19.
Once more, we are in the garden in verse 39.

"Nicodemus came also who had come to him by night bringing a mixture of myrrh and aloes about 100 pounds in weight."

Myrrh in the Bible was used for one thing: anointing a corpse for burial. When Jesus was born, they brought gold because He would be a king, they brought incense because He would be a priest, but they brought myrrh because he would die. Remember the church at Smyrna, that Jesus told them *"Satan will put you in prison for ten days, and kill some of you?"* Myrrh, or *smyrna* in Greek.

"And, so they took the body of Jesus and bound it in linen wrapping with the spices, as was the burial custom of the Jews. Now, in the place where He was crucified, there was a garden."

It had to be in a garden, same as Genesis, same as Gethsemane.

"In the place He was crucified, there was a garden. And, in the garden, a new tomb in which no one had yet been laid. Therefore, on account of the Jewish day of preparation, because the tomb was nearby, they laid Jesus there."

Jesus was buried in a garden. The previous day, the Saturday, they were reading *Ha Shit Hashirim*. To this day in the synagogue on that Saturday of *Ha Matzot*, Passover week, you read *Megilla*, known to you as the Song of Solomon. Turn with me to the Song of Solomon, 4:6 please.

"Until the cool of the day, when the shadow flees away, I will go to the mountain of myrrh and to the hill of frankincense."

The bridegroom was anointed for burial, to die for the bride; to bring the acceptable sacrifice. Solomon's romance with the shulammite is a metaphor of Christ's romance with the church. He is anointed for burial, to die for His bride. That is what was being read in the Synagogue.

Now look at Song of Solomon 5:1: *"I have come in to my garden, my sister, my bride. I've gathered my myrrh along with my balsam."* To put it another way, "Come on in. Come on in to the garden." That is what is being read in the synagogue on the Saturday.

The next day, Sunday, the first day of the week, is called in Hebrew *yom Rishon*. That *yom Rishon*, however, was a unique *yom Rishon* in the

Jewish calendar. It is the Hebrew Feast of First Fruits.

Turn to 1 Corinthians 15:20. The resurrection chapter, and what do we read? *"But now the Messiah has been raised from the dead, the first fruits of those who are asleep."* Notice "asleep". *"He will bruise you in the head. You'll only bruise him in the heel."* When you go to sleep, you wake up again. As we always point out, the Bible never speaks of the death of a believer as death, but as sleep. Lazarus is asleep. The little girl is asleep; Talitha Tekumi, she's asleep. Paul says *"do not be overly grieved for the brethren who are asleep."* Unsaved people die; believers go to sleep. There is much we can say about this: There are two reasons that the Bible describes the death of a believer as sleep. The first is obviously the resurrection; you wake up again. When you go to sleep, the next thing you are aware of is when you awake. The next thing believers who fall asleep will be aware of in time is the Resurrection. But something else happens when you go to sleep: Your consciousness enters a different sphere, where things that make no sense in our waking hours add up. When you're dreaming, you can dream of dead people alive again, and talk to them. In a dream, you can see past events in the present, and future events in the present. Past, present and future become the same. There is a chronology, but there's no time. We have two Greek words for time, *chronos* and *kairos*. In eternity you only have *chronos*, not *kairos*. In other words, eternity is not a clock that keeps going, but no clock at all. It is *chronos*, chronology, an order of events, but there is no time.

In a dream you can see past events happening again: You can see George Washington crossing the Delaware. You can see anything. You can see something is going to happen, you can dream about your coming vacation to California or whatever. You can dream about things that haven't happened yet. You can see dead people alive, or what happened in Revelation. The lamb was slain before the foundation of the world. He saw the 24 elders on the throne; he saw future events that didn't happen yet happening in the here and now. When you go to sleep you dream, physiologists know we all dream. They know from encephalograms and alpha brain waves among other things, we all dream.

Your consciousness enters a different sphere where things that would make no sense in the waking hours, they make sense, that's what happens when you die. So, the question becomes, well, does your soul go to sleep, or do you go to be with the Lord? Relative to us, you're in your grave. Relative to eternity, it's already happening. It says in Ephesians 2:6 that we're already seated with Christ in the heavenly places. You cannot apply time to eternity. That's one of the first places the Calvinists go wrong, they try to apply time to eternity. Is there eternal security? Yes. Because in eternity, it's already happening, but eternal security in the Bible does not mean once saved, always saved. To us, it's a variable. There is eternal security, but not in the way the Calvinists think there is. They muddle everything on that. Calvinism is based on humanism. It is humanism. It's crazy.

But believers go to sleep. Christ is the first fruits of those who are asleep. This is the messianic fulfilment of the Hebrew Feast of First Fruits. What would happen on this Sunday, *yom Rishon*, of First Fruits?—that Sunday of Passover week? That Saturday on which they had read the Song of Solomon and still do to this day? The Sunday before dawn, while it was still dark, the high priest would descend from the temple into the Kidron Valley, where he would wait for the first ray of light to come from behind of the Mount of Olives. When he saw the first pin of sunlight, he would ceremonially harvest the first stalks of grain of the spring harvest and ceremonially harvest them. That would be called the First Fruit.

Now all four gospels tell us Jesus rose at sunrise. As I've often pointed out, the rising of the s-u-n is a metaphor in biblical philology for the rising of the S-o-n. Even the Old Testament in Isaiah 60:1 says, *"arise and shine for your light has come. The glory of the risen Lord is brighter than the sun,"* etc. All four gospels say the resurrection was just at the very crack of dawn, while it was still dark. The very hour, of the very day of the year when the high priest was bringing the first fruit into the temple, harvesting the first fruit, Jesus arose as the first fruit of the resurrection.

In a garden! So, let's see again what happens in the garden. Man falls in the garden, the curse is placed on man in the garden, but then in the garden, that same God takes our sin and is arrested for it. Then in a garden, He's crucified for it. In the place He was crucified, there was a garden. He's crucified in our place in the garden. But then something else happens in the garden.

John, Chapter 20:1.

Now the first day of the week, (yom Rishon, the Hebrew Feast of

First Fruits) **Mary Magdalene,** (Mary Magdala—she came from Magdol in Galilee, which would have meant it was a place where there was a tower) **came early to the tomb while it was still dark.** (Same as the high priest had to go into the garden when it was still dark) **she saw the stone already taken away from the tomb, so she ran and came to Simon Peter and to the other disciple whom Jesus loved, and said to them, "They've taken away the Lord out of the tomb. We don't know where they've laid Him."**

Notice, the bad news in the garden came to a woman first. The curse came upon a woman first. The bad news came on a woman first. So the good news had to come to a woman first. You understand why it had to be a woman? It couldn't be a man; it had to be a woman. The curse came on a woman first, so the good news had to come to the woman first.

"Peter, therefore, went, and the other disciples, and they were going to the tomb. And the two were running together and the other disciple ran ahead faster than Peter and came to the tomb first. And stooping in and looking in, he saw the linen wrappings lying there, but he didn't go in. Simon Peter therefore also came following him and entered the tomb, and he beheld the linen wrappings lying there. And the face cloth, which had been on his head, not lying with the linen wrappings, but rolled up in a place by itself."

Now, this is a cultural nuance. Carpenters in biblical times in the ancient Near East, when they were given a commission to build something, or to complete something, they would hang a cloth. At the end of the day, they would use the cloth to remove perspiration. But at the end of the day, when the work was finished, the cloth, or napkin, would be folded and left there.

"So, the other disciple who had come to the tomb, entered then also. And he saw and believed. For as yet, they did not understand the Scripture, that He must rise again from the dead. So the disciples went away again to their homes. But Mary was standing outside the tomb weeping; and so as she wept, she stooped and looked into the tomb. And beheld two angels in white sitting, one at the head and one at the feet, where the body of Jesus had been lying."

Now, again, these two angels correspond to the two cherubs on the Ark of the Covenant, but I'm not going to go into that, now. You can get the tapes if you're interested.

"And they said to her, 'Woman, why are you weeping?' And she said to them, Because they have taken away my Lord, and I don't know where they have laid Him. When she said this, she turned around and beheld Jesus standing there and didn't know it was Jesus. Jesus said to her, 'Woman, why are you weeping? Whom are you seeking?' Supposing Him to be the gardener."

Now, what was the gardener saying the previous day in the Song of Solomon? *"Come into my garden my beloved."* You see, in Genesis, the angel said, get out of here. Get out of the garden, you can't come in anymore. But once He took our sin in the garden and was raised from the dead, now the angel says, *"Come on in. Come on in. He is risen! Come on in."*

Women are more sensitive. They get it first. Men are bit thick in the head. So the story continues. She tries to tell the apostles.

"Supposing Him to be the gardener, she said to him, 'Sir, if you've carried Him away, tell me where you have laid Him and I will take Him away.' But Jesus said to her, 'Mary.' And she turned to Him [and said in Hebrew, which would have actually been the Hebrew dialect of Aramaic] Rabboni, (which means my Teacher). Jesus said to her, 'Stop clinging to me. For I have not ascended to my Father. But go to my brethren and say to them, I ascend to my Father and your Father, to my God and your God.'"

In John's gospel, previously, Jesus referred to the Father as His Father, in the possessive personal possessive. Once He took our sin and rose from the dead, now He is our Father.

"Mary Magdalene came announcing to the disciples" (women get it first, I'm convinced of this issue. Eight out of ten times when a husband and wife get saved, it's the wife who gets saved first). "'I've seen the Lord,' and that He had said these things to her. When therefore it was evening on that day, the first day of the week (the Jews count days sundown to sundown) when the doors were shut, the disciples were assembled for fear of the Jews, Jesus came and stood in their midst and said to them, (shalom alechem,) peace be with you".

Now, when it says "fear of the Jews" it means Judeans. It doesn't refer to the people being Jewish. They were all Jewish. Jesus was Jewish. They were all Jewish. Mary was Jewish, the apostles were Jewish. What you have here is a translation issue of the Greek word yudeioi it means the Judeans. The religious establishment in and around Jerusalem and the people they controlled. It doesn't mean ethnic Jews, because they're all Jews. It meant the religious establishment in and around Jerusalem, the Sanhedrin and those who they controlled.

And He says, *"Peace be with you."* I've explained this various times, but we have people who have not heard it before. I live in England where doctor Samuel Johnson sardonically, yet accurately, in his dictionary, defined peace as a period of preparation and deception between two wars. We think of peace in the Greek sense of being "Irene," like the girl's name; an absence of conflict. That's peace as the world gives you. God's peace is shalom. Now, ultimately, His peace will include an absence of conflict. When Jesus returns, the nations will beat their spears into pruning hooks. Ultimately shalom will include an absence of conflict. But an absence of conflict is not shalom. Shalom comes from the infinitive of the Hebrew verb, *leshalem*. *Leshaleru* means to pay. It is a synonym in biblical Hebrew for the word *le malot*, meaning to fill. It's not in the modern Hebrew, but in biblical Hebrew, it's to fill. It's a synonym. And it's to fulfil. *Leshalem*, the word shalom comes from *leshalem*. We get shalom from *leshaleru*, to pay, to fill, and to fulfil. We have shalom because Jesus came to pay the price for our sin, to fill us with His spirit, and to fulfil the law, the torah. We have shalom because the Messiah came to *leshaleru*, to pay the price for our sin, to fill us with his spirit and to fulfil the law. You can be in the biggest conflict of your life and have shalom. Or you can be in a perfectly pristine circumstance and lack it. Yeshua said, *"My peace I give to you. Not like the world gives you."*

"My peace." That's what He said.

Now, the obvious question is this: In the garden we blew it. In the garden Satan conned us and he is conning to this day. In the garden we bought a curse on ourselves. But in the garden God promised redemption. Whether you believe it or not is irrelevant. It's appointed to man once to die and after this the judgment. If you don't believe what I'm saying today, I guarantee you a time will come when you will believe it. But it will be too late. The only issue is, is it true or false? I can tell you it is true. You'll believe it someday. But it will be too late. Now is the appointed time, today is the day of salvation.

Just like Adam and Eve, you are standing naked before a holy perfect God. And all the fig leaves in the world are not good enough. No amount of fig leaves can save you from the wrath of God. You may be trusting in good works and being what society calls a good person. No matter how good you are, you are not good enough to go to Heaven. No matter how good you are, you're not good enough to not go to Hell. But no matter how bad you are, you are not so bad that God doesn't love you and doesn't want to save you.

See, I had an advantage. I didn't grow up in a Protestant culture. I didn't even know what a born-again Christian was. By the time I was sixteen, I was fooling around with heroin. I didn't know. Nobody had to convince me I was a sinner. I already knew that. The devil gets more people into Hell with religion than he does all the dope, all the immorality, all the gambling, all of these type sins put together. Fig leaves populate Hell. So, you're standing naked before your maker and you may be sewing fig leaves together. You're trusting religion. Without the shedding of blood, there's no forgiveness of sin.

But somebody came into that garden in your place. Just think of a trial where there's a judge, a prosecutor and a defence attorney. Now, either that judge and that prosecutor and that defence attorney are going to be for you or against you. Suppose you're at this trial where that judge was also your defence attorney. You couldn't lose. Where the prosecutor was Satan, the accuser of the brethren. If that judge is also your defence attorney and the prosecutor is Satan, you can't lose. On the other hand, if that judge is not your defence attorney, but he's your prosecutor, you can't win.

But you can win. How? By letting Him take your sin. In the garden He already took it. You just have to accept that He did it. That's the gospel. He already took it—you just have to accept that He did it. Fig leaves will do you no good. Sacraments, novenas, religion, won't do you any good. Those are fig leaves. I'm not against good works. We do good works because we've been saved—not to get saved. It happened in the garden. That's your choice. He took your sin. You can turn from sin and ask Him to forgive you. Ask Him to come into your life and give you a new life. He can make you Barabbas. He did this, she did that. Yeah, I know. But now there is the Son of the Father. Take me instead. He saw you under the fig tree. He wants to say to you what He said to His disciples. In fact, He wants to say to you what He said to me. What He said to His disciples, He wants to say to us because He wants us to be His disciples. He said to them, "Peace be unto you." *Shalom alechem.*

You want shalom? No problem. You can have it. You can have shalom because I came to *leshaleru,* in the garden, to pay the price for your sin. To fill you with my spirit, and to fulfil the law of God you could never begin to keep. That's what Jesus said to Mary Magdalene, that's what Jesus said to Peter, James, and John. That's what Jesus said to me. And if you're not born again, it's what He wants to say to you today. *Shalom alechem.*

If you don't know Him, find out. Talk to a Christian and don't rest until you hear Jesus tell you *shalom alechem.* God bless.

Hope for the Hopeless

I N this message, dear friends, we will be looking at Hebrews chapter 11; most of us are familiar with this passage of scripture as the "faith chapter". Indeed, we have a teaching on it called Emunah , the Judeo- Christian understanding of faith. Faith is certainly one main aspect of this chapter, but there is another main idea we are given here that will be our focus in this letter: hope. Hebrews 11 has as much to do with hope as it does with faith.

The book of Hebrews was written to Jewish Christians in and around Jerusalem before the second temple was destroyed in 70 AD. Up until this time, the believers had been persecuted almost exclusively by the Sanhedrin and the rabbinic establishment. In other words, there were believing Jews whom unbelieving Jews were persecuting. However, something began to happen at this time, probably around the time of Nero's reign as emperor of Rome. For the first time, believers were not only persecuted by unbelieving Jews, but also by the Roman government – or, at the very least, they were faced with the prospect of it. Nero is the emperor who killed both Peter and Paul, according to Eusebius and the historical record. There was a resulting danger of some people being tempted to go back under the law in order to escape persecution. Many of them were distraught because they foresaw the destruction and judgment coming on Jerusalem, remembering the prophecies of Daniel as well as of Jesus himself.

That is the backdrop against which the book of Hebrews was written. In it, therefore, the author addresses the situation in this chapter by dealing with two subjects: one is faith, the other is hope. What we will do here is to first look through this chapter, talking about the nuances and background, and then we'll think about what it means for us.

Beginning in verse 1 of Hebrews 11:

> "Faith is the assurance of things hoped for, the conviction of things not seen".

The word "assurance" there, sometimes translated from Greek as "substance", is *hypostases*. Faith and hope, we see here, go hand-in-hand. The Hebrew and Greek words are interesting; the word for "faith" in Greek is *pistes* or *piston,* and in Hebrew *emunah.* In both languages, this is not only the word for "faith", but also for "faithfulness". *"The righteous shall live by faith"–"The righteous shall live by faithfulness". "Without faith it is impossible to please God"–"Without faithfulness it is impossible to please God"* Hebrews 11:6 . We are saved by grace through faith, and also through faithfulness – beginning, of course, with the faithfulness of Jesus.

But then there is "hope"–*Tigna.* In Greek, *elpis.* Look once again at what it tells us: *"Faith is the assurance of things hoped for".* You cannot define biblical faith unless you do it in light of hope, nor can you define biblical hope unless you define it in light of faith. We think of "I hope" as being synonymous with "I wish". In the Bible, however, that is not the case; rather hope in biblical terms is a future fact. We have faith in a future fact. Faith is the assurance of our hope – we are assured that it will happen. Religions cannot give people the assurance of salvation, and that includes unbiblical forms of Christianity. Only the Lord Jesus can give us that assurance.

We have a hope, and that hope is not "I wish this would happen", but knowing and trusting that it will happen.

Let us continue with verses 2 and 3:

> "For by it the men of old gained approval. By faith we understand that the worlds were prepared by the Word of God, so that what is seen was not made out of things which are visible."

He begins a historical account all the way back from creation up to the time of King David – the reason it ends with David is that the Messiah would be seen not only as a prophet like Moses (Deut.) but also as a king like David. Their national aspiration as Jews was for the

Messiah to come as the son of David and restore what they had lost in the Babylonian captivity.

The account begins, however, with creation, telling us that by faith we believe that God made the things that are from the things that are not – by his Word. When it says "his Word", it is, of course, *ho Logos* in Greek, or Jesus. Jesus is the Word made flesh, as John 1 tells us. If you don't believe the Bible, you don't believe in Jesus Christ. The things outside of what Jesus said and of the rest of scripture are just religious nonsense. Someone gave me a silly note this morning with religious nonsense in it, saying that "as long as we are seeking spirituality we are saved". This is New Age idiocy, certainly not the gospel of Jesus. Only an unsaved person would write something so silly, and I do feel sorry for them. But this is what many people think, despite the fact that it's nonsense.

Only God can violate the law of conservation of matter and the law of conservation of energy – otherwise he wouldn't be God. Only God can make something out of nothing. By faith we understand that the worlds were prepared by the Word of God; we see Jesus in the creation in John chapter 1 verse 3: *"The world was made through him, and without him nothing was made that was made."*

We also see Jesus in the creation in Proverbs 8. Adam heard God walking in the garden – that was Jesus, he was there from day one. So it begins with him in the creation.

After this, in verse 4 of Hebrews 11, it says this:

"By faith Abel offered to God a sacrifice that was better than Cain's, through which he obtained the testimony that he was righteous, God testifying about his gifts; that through faith though he is dead he still speaks."

So we see that the next phase spoken of is the time directly following the fall of mankind. Abel is the first martyr; Jesus spoke of him as such in Matthew 23, saying to the religious hypocrites of his day that *"the blood of the martyrs will be upon you from Abel"*. Again, think of the Bible the way you would think of an unsliced loaf of bread, fresh from a baker's oven: it looks the same from both ends. In both Revelation and Genesis, you have the woman and the stars, the tree of Life, and the serpent; in Genesis it says *"the blood of your brother cries out"*, speaking of Abel, and in Revelation it says, *"the blood of the martyrs cries out"*. Genesis and Revelation work hand in hand; the Bible ends the same way it begins, with the same imagery. We have the creation, the new creation, and finally the re-creation.

So we have Abel, still speaking. The righteous men of old still speak – Isaiah, Jeremiah, and Ezekiel all still speak. They speak to Israel and also to the church. Peter, James, John, and Paul also continue to speak to us through the Word. The things that Isaiah, Amos, the apostles, Moses, and all the other authors of scripture wrote are every bit as much for us today as they were for the people living at the time the prophets and apostles were writing it. In fact, many things are even more for us today. The Bible is the Word of God in the word of man; that's what we must understand about the Word.

Jesus was one hundred percent human and one hundred percent divine; just so, the Word of God is in the word of man. The Bible is one hundred percent God's Word, but it is also one hundred percent man's word. Just as Jesus was God and Man, so the Bible is the Word of God in the word of man. These great heroes and champions of faith from the Old Testament and from the apostolic church still speak to us today. You will find as you read Isaiah or Jeremiah that what they said applies to us today.

Let us continue with verse 5:

> "By faith Enoch was taken up, so that he did not see death, 'and was not found, because God had taken him'; for before he was taken he had this testimony, that he pleased God."

Enoch is the first man who was ever raptured. Every rapture experience in the Bible is a type or a foreshadow of the rapture of the church – the rapture of Elijah, what happened to Paul which he described in 2 Corinthians, what happened to John in Revelation 4:1, the ascension of Jesus, and first the rapture of Enoch – all these things are pictures of the rapture that is coming. They teach something about that ultimate rapture of God's people. The catholic church has invented one that is not in the Bible, of course – the rapture of Mary – which has no biblical basis whatsoever.

So the retelling of history continues with Enoch, the first person who was ever raptured. This occasion was antediluvian, or before the flood.

The text continues, saying the following in verse 6:35

> "But without faith" (that is, without faithfulness) "it is impossible to

please Him, for he who comes to God must believe that He is, and that He is a rewarder of those who diligently seek Him."

This idea of reward comes into play later on in the chapter. You see, in order to be saved, to be a Christian and to go to heaven, it is not enough to believe that God is. Believing that He is, is certainly necessary, but in itself that is not sufficient. It is not even enough to believe that God is a righteous Judge who will judge sin; not enough to believe that you are condemned and on your way to hell. None of it is enough unless you put your faith in Jesus Christ. You must believe that God is, yes; but you must also believe that God is the rewarder. In other words, in order to go to heaven you must believe that there is such a place and that God wants you to get there; you must believe that He is a rewarder.

After Enoch, we move into the next age (Hebrews 11:7) –

"By faith Noah, being divinely warned of things not yet seen, moved with godly fear, prepared an ark for the saving of his household, by which he condemned the world and became heir of the righteousness which is according to faith."

Here, of course, we have the deluge, and the faithful one is none other than Noah. Was Noah a successful preacher? No, not by the world's standards. Seven people, eight including himself, were saved through his message – and those seven were all related to him.

We have a tape entitled "Just as it was in the days of Noah", which explains how the Last Days will be the same as were the days of Noah; we also go into it on the "Preparing for Persecution" tapes. God is in the business of saving families; however, He also tells us that just as Noah's warning was rejected, so in the Last Days will ours be when the true believers try to warn unbelievers of the coming judgment and destruction. We will not be believed until it is too late, which is exactly what happened to Noah. However, just as his family made it to safety in the ark, so those in the true church will indeed make it out of here.

The passage continues with Abraham (Hebrews 11:8-10) –

"By faith Abraham obeyed when he was called to go out to the place which he would receive as an inheritance. And he went out, not knowing where he was going. By faith he dwelt in the land of promise as in a foreign country, dwelling in tents with Isaac and Jacob, the heirs with him of the same promise; for he waited for the city which has foundations, whose builder and maker is God."

Here the passage goes into the patriarchal period, naming the Patriarchs: Abraham, Isaac, and Jacob. There are others as well, as we will see in a moment. It says that Abraham left the place where he was for another destination, not knowing where he was going. We must understand the background: Daniel said that the Messiah would come and die before the second temple was destroyed (Daniel 9:26). The people to whom the book of Hebrews was addressed knew that the Messiah had come and died; therefore, the city and the temple would soon be destroyed. Jesus warned them in the Olivet Discourse to flee when they saw Jerusalem surrounded by an army of gentiles (Luke 21:20,21, Matthew 24:15-20). What the writer of Hebrews is saying here, in part, is to look at the faith and the faithfulness of the men of old.

When Abraham was told to leave his home, he left for a destination unknown to him; he was searching for a better city, and he went out by faith. "Don't hold on to this city" is the message that the writer of Hebrews was getting at for the Jewish believers in Jerusalem. These believers in 70AD, under a cousin of Jesus named Simeon, actually did flee from Jerusalem and were rescued. Their message of warning to Jerusalem had been rejected, its citizens choosing to believe the rabbis instead. As a result they were destroyed. Simeon, who became pastor of the church at Jerusalem after the apostle James was martyred, left with his church. This can be verified in reading Josephus and Eusebius, and once again, this is a major type or picture of the rapture. This will happen again in the Last Days, though of course it will then occur on a grander scale.

So the writer of Hebrews is saying, "Look at Abraham. He had to leave his home too. Don't worry about this city; God has a better Jerusalem. Don't be attached to this Jerusalem; there is a heavenly Jerusalem." Earlier in the book he tells us that the temple and the things within it were only shadows, or types, of the ones in heaven (Hebrews 9).

The author of Hebrews is also telling believers here that just as Abraham lived in a land promised to him, so we ought to live in this world. *"The meek shall inherit the earth"* (Matthew 5:5). This will happen during the millennial reign of Jesus; there is no doubt that we will inherit it. Therefore, just as Abraham lived as a sojourner or a foreigner in a land promised to him, so should we live in this world.

We are promised this place – we will co-reign with Christ during the millennium. In the meantime, however, we live as sojourners and foreigners in this land that we actually own.

There are people today who are caught up in a lot of nonsense involving Kingdom-Now Theology and Dominionism; that is not what this is about. The ideas that Satan is already bound and that we are going to "conquer the world for Christ before He comes" are silly nonsense and absolute rubbish – Jesus told us that His kingdom is not of this world, and as you may have heard me say before, if Satan is now bound I would like to know who keeps letting him go.

Nonetheless, look at Abraham. He was waiting for a better city, living in a land that was promised to him. So should we; the heavenly Jerusalem is ours, and we will inherit the earth. Augustine of Hippo later borrowed this theme when the Visigoths were going to destroy Rome in the fourth century. He wrote something then that he called "City of God" – which I've never really been impressed with – taking the theme of Hebrews 11, as if he was trying to write a sequel to it.

Let us continue with Hebrews 11:11-13:

> "By faith Sarah herself also received strength to conceive seed, and she bore a child when she was past the age, because she judged Him faithful who had promised. Therefore from one man, and him as good as dead, were born as many as the stars of the sky in multitude – innumerable as the sand, which is by the seashore. These all died in faith, not having received the promises, but having seen them afar off were assured of them, embraced them and confessed that they were strangers and pilgrims on the earth."

Here we are introduced to the first woman in this list – Sarah, wife of Abraham, mother of Isaac. Verse 13 says that these people saw these things from a distance; more specifically, they only saw the first coming of Jesus at a distance. We now have His first coming, and we see His second coming from a distance. So in the same way they looked forward to His first coming, while not actually experiencing that redemption in their own lives, we should look forward to His second coming. This is what the text is telling us. His second coming is our certain hope, just as His first coming was to those listed in the passage.

The text continues (Hebrews 11:14-16):

> "For those who say such things declare plainly that they seek a homeland. And truly if they had called to mind that country from which they had come out, they would have had opportunity to return. But now they desire a better, that is, a heavenly country. Therefore God is not ashamed to be called their God, for He has prepared a city for them."

By definition, backsliding is trusting in this world, or looking for something here. Most of the seductions being perpetrated by Satan against the modern church are designed to entice us to trust in this world. This applies equally to Faith-Prosperity, Kingdom-Now, and all other deceptions that are designed to get God's people to trust in this world rather than in the coming one.

Look at the kinds of things they say: "God wants you rich, you're a king's kid, name-it-and-claim-it, blab-it-and-grab-it, look for your blessing here, don't worry about the heavenly mansion, claim your mansion now". All these things are custom-made to seduce us into trusting in this life. Yet we are told to be like the ones in Hebrews 11, who kept looking for the good that God had promised.

Continuing in verses 17-19:

> "By faith Abraham, when he was tested, offered up Isaac, and he who had received the promises offered up his only begotten son, of whom it was said, 'In Isaac your seed shall be called,' concluding that God was able to raise him up, even from the dead, from which he also received him in a figurative sense."

Again, these people saw the gospel from a distance. Abraham is called *Yedid Yah*, the "friend of God". As you may have heard me say, in the times of the Old Testament the Holy Spirit was reserved for certain people at certain times with certain functions: patriarchs, high priests, kings, and prophets. The Holy Spirit was not then for all who believed; that is peculiar to the New Covenant.

By the Holy Spirit, however, these chosen people knew certain things. Abraham knew that God had promised to fulfil His Word to him through his son Isaac, so that even if Isaac died he would receive him back again. This, of course, is an obvious type – Abraham giving up his only begotten son (in Greek *monogenes*) just as God would give up His only begotten Son.

However, God tells Abraham to take his "only begotten son", meaning Isaac. Where is Ishmael? God does not recognise Ishmael as

Abraham's begotten son; He never recognises anything that is done in the flesh. There is a big difference between a good thing and a God thing. There are many people today who are doing "good" things that are not "God" things; for example, there are people who call themselves Christian missionaries, but who have only social gospels. This means they spend their time trying to meet people's humanitarian needs without giving them the message of salvation. I see this all the time with organisations that try to "bless" Israel, yet withhold Christ from the Jews. They may be doing a "good" thing, but they are certainly not doing a God thing; therefore these organisations are biblically useless and not of God. What is it when people do these kinds of things? It is the creation of Ishmaels. God recognises nothing that is done in the flesh, even though it may be done with the right motive. We must learn to be motivated by the Lord, not by needs.

We saw that verse 19 says that Abraham considered God able to raise his son even from the dead. What this meant to the believers who were reading it is this: "Look, just as God had a promise for Isaac, so in Christ does God have a promise for us. Even if you should die in persecution, don't worry – just as Abraham knew that God was able to raise Isaac from the dead, so must you know that He is able to raise you from the dead. God is faithful. Abraham was unafraid to see Isaac die, and you can also be unafraid to die because God will raise you up again." Why didn't these people, the believers we are told about in both Old and New Testaments, see the things that were promised to them? Because God wanted us to be a part of things also. Why did the patriarchs die without seeing the coming of Jesus? Because God wanted to save us as well. But at the resurrection, it all finally happens together, with no one left out.

Continuing in verse 20 of Hebrews 11:

"By faith Isaac blessed Jacob and Esau concerning things to come."

As we discuss on the 'Jewish-Arab Reconciliation in Christ' tape, God has a blessing and a prophetic purpose for the Arab nations just as He does for the Jewish nation. Verse 21:

"By faith Jacob, when he was dying, blessed each of the sons of Joseph, and worshipped, leaning on the top of his staff."

This story is found in Genesis 49, where we see the twelve sons of

Jacob just as again we see them in Revelation 7 and 14 as the 12 tribes of Israel – the loaf of bread once more, that looks alike at both ends. In verse 22 we read this:

> "By faith Joseph, when he was dying, made mention of the departure of the children of Israel, and gave instructions concerning his bones."

The final patriarchal figure becomes Joseph, who gives instruction about his bones. As most of you know, the Exodus of Israel is a picture of two things: First, it is a picture of our salvation. Egypt is a figure of the world, Pharaoh a figure of the god of this world, Satan. As Moses made a covenant with the blood of the lamb, sprinkling it on the people and bringing them out of Egypt, through the Red Sea and into the Promised Land, so Jesus made a covenant with the blood of the Lamb – His own blood – and leads us out of the world, through baptism, and into Heaven. One is a picture of the other.

However, the Exodus is also a picture of the rapture and resurrection. The same judgments that God sends on Egypt – blood, pestilence, darkness, hail – are also in the book of Revelation. As you may have heard me point out, in the same way that Pharaoh's magicians counterfeited the miracles of Moses and Aaron, so the Antichrist and the false prophet will counterfeit the miracles of Jesus and His witnesses. When the people of Israel came out of Egypt, they were rescued – that is a picture of the rapture of the church. However, in the Exodus they also brought Joseph's bones with them (Exodus 13:19). Why? Because the dead in Christ will rise first! (I Thessalonians 4:16). So just as Joseph's bones came out of Egypt with the Israelites, the dead in Christ and those who are alive at His coming will escape this world together. The writer of Hebrews is saying that those to whom he is writing should not be afraid to die in the persecution for these reasons.

With these verses we come to the phase of the Exodus. Verse 23 of Hebrews 11:

> "By faith Moses, when he was born, was hidden three months by his parents, because they saw he was a beautiful child; and they were not afraid of the king's command. By faith Moses, when he became of age, refused to be called the son of Pharaoh's daughter, choosing rather to suffer affliction with the people of God than to enjoy the passing pleasures of sin, esteeming the reproach of Christ" – the Messiah –

"greater treasures than the riches in Egypt; for he looked to the reward. By faith he forsook Egypt, not fearing the wrath of the king; for he endured as seeing Him who is invisible. By faith he kept the Passover and the sprinkling of blood, lest he who destroyed the firstborn should touch them. By faith they passed through the Red Sea as by dry land, whereas the Egyptians, attempting to do so, were drowned."

Moses, of course, is a type of Christ in many ways. God promised that the Messiah would be a prophet like Moses (Deuteronomy 18:15-19); both Moses and Jesus ushered in a covenant of God with His people. The first time Moses came to save the Jews, he was rejected by them; they only accepted him the second time. In the meantime, Moses lived among the Gentiles as a shepherd. He is a foreshadow of Jesus, who when He came the first time to the Jews was rejected by them. Jesus therefore went to the Gentiles, just as Moses had done. The second time Jesus comes, however, He will be accepted by Israel, as seen in the book of Zechariah.

Moses was a prince of Egypt; he could have had a good life in this world. However, he chose instead to face hardship. He chose to lead a difficult life rather than be enticed by the fleeting pleasures of sin. He was looking forward to the coming of the Messiah. So we see that the next thing the writer of Hebrews is saying to the church in Jerusalem around 70 AD is this: Pharaoh is comparable to the Roman emperor, specifically Nero – Moses was not afraid of the king, so why should you be as believers? You are being tempted to go back under the law, to compromise so that you can have a good life in this world, but look at Moses. He could have done that, he could have had a really comfortable life as a prince of Egypt – but he did not trust this world, rather looking forward to the Messiah's coming. Therefore you must look forward to Messiah's second coming; be like Moses.

The next phase in Israel's history is the one, which we call the Conquest. Interestingly, Hebrews alludes to Joshua, but does not name him; instead it names a Gentile woman, who was, of all things, a prostitute: Rahab. Let's examine the scripture (Hebrews 11:30,31):

"By faith the walls of Jericho fell down after they were encircled for seven days. By faith the harlot Rahab did not perish with those who did not believe, when she had received the spies with peace."

The text here points out the seven days during which Jericho was surrounded. It does this for a reason: the rescue of Rahab is once again a major picture of the rapture of the church. It points us back to Joshua 6; a Jewish Christian reading the book of Revelation at the end of the first century or the beginning of the second would have called Revelation chapters 8 through 11 a Midrash on the book of Joshua. If you remember, Hebrews points out the seven days of Israel's campaign against Jericho, during which there had to be silence. According to Revelation 8, there is silence in heaven also. In the book of Joshua we see that Israel marched around Jericho for seven days, but on the seventh day they marched around seven times. Following the same numerical pattern, there are seven seals in the book of Revelation, followed by a subset of seven trumpets opening up from the seventh seal.

Then you have the last trumpet in Joshua: when they blow the trumpet, it says in Joshua that the city was given to them by the Lord. The trumpet we see here is all wrapped up in the symbolism of the year of Jubilee and the Hebrew Feast of Trumpets – this is all complicated, and we do have tapes to specifically explain these things, though I do not have time to address them now. At the last trumpet in Revelation, Christ returns, and this is all also linked with the book of Joel and many other things. However, we will only deal with it now in so far as it deals with our subject–again, when the last trumpet is blown in Joshua, the walls come down and then the Lord gives the city to Israel. In Revelation, when the last trumpet is blown, the text tells us *"this world has become the kingdom of our God and of His Messiah."* (Revelation 11:15). One is a picture of the other.

Hebrews also makes mention of two witnesses, paralleled in Joshua by the two spies. Somehow the two spies in Joshua are types or foreshadows of the two witnesses in Revelation. There are many examples in the Bible who teach concerning those two witnesses; people often wonder whether they are Moses and Elijah or Moses and Enoch or Moses and the Apostle John – people always ask who they are, but really there are many, many different ones who foreshadow these two witnesses. The two spies in Joshua is one example.

The reason that scripture speaks of Rahab and her rescue, again, is pointing to the rescue of the church that would happen in 70 AD, but ultimately to the rapture of the church of which that rescue was a picture. We should always look to the rapture and the return of Jesus as our hope, not becoming worried about persecution or opposition.

The way in which the Lord effected the rescue of His people in the past is the same way He will effect our rescue. Our ultimate hope is to be rescued by Jesus from this planet when He comes back.

Hebrews does not mention Joshua directly in this passage, but instead refers to the Gentile woman whom he rescued. It is always interesting to see Gentiles listed in the genealogies of Jesus, who was of the house of David; David's house began with the union of a Jewish man with a Gentile woman – Boaz and Ruth. Jesus came from a union of Jew and Gentile because He would be the Saviour of both Jew and Gentile; that is the picture being painted by the inclusion of non-Jews, which goes back again to Abraham. Abraham was both a Jew and a Gentile: he was born a Gentile, but was converted by God to Judaism. He could be the father of all who believe because he was both Jew and Gentile; the Messiah would save both Jew and Gentile. This kind of imagery is present right from the beginning – Noah, Enoch, and Abel were all Gentiles. From the very beginning, God's plan was for the salvation of all mankind; the Jews were simply to be His vehicle to bring it to the nations.

Let us continue with Hebrews 11:32:

> "And what more shall I say? For the time would fail me to tell of Gideon and Barak and Samson and Jephthah, also of David and Samuel and the prophets:"

After Rahab, we find that the writer moves on to the period of the Judges, naming Samson, Jephthah, Barak, and Gideon. The period following Judges in biblical history is generally referred to as the period of Prophets and Kings; named here are Samuel and King David. We will look at these in more detail a little further on. Moving on to verses 33 - 36:

> "who through faith subdued kingdoms, worked righteousness, obtained promises, stopped the mouths of lions, quenched the violence of fire, escaped the edge of the sword, out of weakness were made strong, became valiant in battle, turned to flight the armies of the aliens. Women received their dead raised to life again. Others were tortured, not accepting deliverance, that they might obtain a better resurrection. Still others had trial of mockings and scourgings, yes, and of chains and imprisonment."

Torture? Chains? Imprisonment? Beatings? But if you're a king's kid, you don't have to suffer; if you're suffering, that means you don't have enough faith. Well, which faith are you going to believe: The faith of Hebrews 11, which is the faith of the Bible, or the faith of the prosperity preachers? It is not possible to believe both. Continuing in verse 37:

> "They were stoned, they were sawn in two, were tempted, were slain with the sword. They wandered about in" — five thousand dollar suits, chauffeur-driven limousines, and five-star hotels? Oh, wait — for a moment I thought I was in Oklahoma. That's not what it says after all — "They were stoned, they were sawn in two, were tempted, were slain with the sword. They wandered about in sheepskins and goatskins, being destitute, afflicted, tormented — of whom the world was not worthy. They wandered in deserts and mountains, in dens and caves of the earth. And all these, having obtained a good testimony through faith, did not receive the promise, God having provided something better for us, that they should not be made perfect apart from us."

Why did Jesus not return for the early church? Or why did He not come the first time for Abraham, Isaac, and Jacob? Because God did not want to bless them without blessing us also; He wants to include us in His blessing. Of course, this is faith in Jesus we are talking about; the prosperity preachers are teaching faith in faith. You may believe them or you may believe the Bible, but you may not believe both, because they are in direct contradiction. Worship God or worship mammon, but you may not have both. However, this is all included in our teaching on faith, and today we are looking instead at hope.

This passage retells biblical history, from the creation all the way up to king David. The further Israel drifted away from the Word of God, the worse things got; Hebrews uses the people in chapter 11 to exemplify what we should be like. There is a term called 'hagiography', from the Greek word 'hagio', meaning 'holy'. Every religion is hagiographic. The Bible is not so, but religion is. What this means is that every religion elevates its central figures to sanctimonious status, making them superhuman. God, however, does not do that; He tells about people for what they were — their good points and their bad points. When you read about these people in scripture you will find that most of them had severe character flaws of some kind that are told about. Religion, however, reveals none of the bad and exaggerates the good in its heroes. Catholicism does it with canonisation, Greek Orthodoxy does it with icons, and Muslims do it with Mohammed.

What would you think of a man who married a six-year old girl and took her virginity when she was nine? You would probably say he was a paedophile, someone who should be emasculated, a pervert who should be in prison. Mohammed did this: he married a girl named Ayeesha when she was six years old, then took her virginity at the age of nine. So the fact of the matter is that Mohammed was a paedophile, a sex pervert, an outrage; but try telling that to a Muslim! This is hagiography.

What would you say about a man who founded a religious order and had a teaching stating that since Eve was created from Adam's rib and ribs are curved, or crooked, women are predisposed to witchcraft; who then, based upon this teaching, would tie women down naked and gynaecologically torture them with boiling water in order to make them confess to witchcraft in order to justify killing them? The man I refer to is Saint Dominic, who started the Dominican order in the Roman Catholic Church. The Dominicans went on to kill half a million people in the name of their religion, and then the Catholic church canonised this man. Last year in Belgium two Dominican nuns were sentenced for crimes that happened in Rwanda, where they killed 7,000 people. Dominicans are still sadistic murderers today. Or we could look at Ignatius Loyola, the founder of the Jesuits, an order that murdered incredibly high numbers of Christians. The Catholic church, true to form, canonised Ignatius Loyola, calling him a saint.

Catholicism claims that Mary appeared to Saint Dominic, whose sordid history we briefly reviewed above, and gave him the rosary. The rosary was actually brought back from the East by crusaders, who saw Hindus counting prayers on beads to Vishnu. The Mormons love Joseph Smith, a convicted swindler who was eventually executed for his crimes. Brigham Young had 23 wives – how would a man who is already married to other wives get more women to marry him? By marrying children! Practically every one of Brigham Young's wives was a minor when he married her. Here we have another paedophile, admired by Mormons, thanks once again to hagiography. Charles Taze Russell and Judge Rutherford, founders of the Jehovah's Witnesses, were both swindlers. This is hagiography – religion makes these sinful men into saints who can do no wrong. The Bible, by contrast, does not do that. The Bible tells you who and what these people were – sinners who were justified by their faith.

To see how scripture differs from hagiography, let's look again at our list of the heroes of the faith in Hebrews 11: Things started out pretty well with Abel and Enoch; Abel was martyred as a kid, and you really can't find much wrong with him. I suppose if he had grown older he would have messed up too. Enoch was raptured, and nothing bad is said of him either. Then, however, we come to Noah, who got loaded after the flood, embarrassed his family and brought a curse on one of his sons which brought a curse on the Canaanite nation centuries later. Abraham – not once, but twice – was willing to give his wife over sexually to another man. She was his half-sister, so he told half the truth. Already we see that if you and I were to go and get people to be emblems and heroes of our faith, we could probably come up with a list we consider more suitable. God, however, is more honest and more realistic.

Moving on to Isaac, we discover that Isaac did the same thing his father did, being willing to give his wife to another man. We inherit our fallen nature from our parents; we groom our kids not only with our good points but also with our bad points. My little boy is no longer so little, and although there are times when I would like to smack him, I realise it would be like standing in front of a mirror and punching the mirror. I know where he got his attitudes – from me.

Then there's mother Sarah. Look what it says about Sarah in verse 11: *"By faith Sarah herself also received strength to conceive seed, and she bore a child when she was past the age, because she judged Him faithful who had promised."* We're talking about a geriatric pregnancy; she was able to conceive, it says here, because of her faith. Yet when we go back to Genesis, we see that she did not believe then. She laughed – therefore she named her son Isaac, which means 'He shall Laugh'. She thought it was ridiculous; it was a joke to her at first. She lacked faith, but God sees the end from the beginning . *"He who began a good work in you will bring it to completion until the day of Jesus Christ"*, Paul tells us in Philippians 1:6. You see, Genesis tells us what these people were; Hebrews tells us what they became.

We only see what we were and what we are; God sees what we shall be because of faith, because of faithfulness.

Then, however, we go further to Joseph. Talk about rejection! It's one thing when unsaved people don't like you; it's worse when believers don't like you; but when those believers are your own family, you're a three-time loser, Jack! Joseph experienced total rejection. He wound up in the joint for a rape he didn't commit after having been sold into slavery by his brothers.

Then there's Moses, who had a contract on his head. He was a wanted man after he knocked somebody off. He was forced to get out of town, to blow the country; then he showed up again 40 years later. If you were going to get someone to be a role model, you wouldn't choose someone who had a warrant out for his or her arrest for capital murder.

Next, we come to Rahab. All right, she's a Gentile woman; but this woman was the biggest hooker around. If there is hope for her, who is there not hope for?

Then it goes into what from a human perspective would appear to be almost preposterous – the period of the Judges, which we call in Hebrew *ha tekophot ha shophtim*.

Samson is chosen as the first role model of the judges, of all people! How could he have been such a sucker for a babe? I mean, Delilah! This was not a woman who was emotionally vulnerable to him; she was trying to get him knocked off – and he knew it, but still continued to go back to her. Why couldn't he find himself a nice Jewish girl? He had to be nuts.

Jephthah – did you ever know anyone who speaks before he thinks, who continually paints himself into a corner with his mouth? Jephthah is the ultimate example of this; he put himself in a situation where he was obligated to kill his own daughter. Did you ever promise things to God, and then not keep the promise?

Then there's Gideon, who wound up with an army of 300 that had begun with 10,000. In the beginning of the story, he could not have made the cut to be part of those 300 himself; he would have been one of the rejects. He doubted God every five minutes – the most famous example was when he put the fleece out before the Lord. He was walking on eggs all the time, a completely insecure person who was constantly asking God for reassurance that he was in His will. How could a totally insecure person become the leader of an elite army of 300 commandos which could and would defeat an army hundreds of times its size? Would you want an insecure person as the leader of a commando unit? How could you trust someone like that?

Next we come to Barak. Deborah and Jael were the real champions of that story, but Hebrews names Barak rather than either of them. Even when God uses a woman, He will not circumvent male authority. Deborah wore the trousers, and Barak wore the skirt. How unfortunate it is to see a Christian marriage where the wife is the spiritual head of the family, looking after the kids spiritually. She is the one stronger in faith; it should not be like that, yet there are many, many families that are. There are many Baraks running around. When you read about him in the book of Judges, you say that guy was a wimp; it was the woman who had the *chutzpah*.

Then we get down to Samuel, who only became what he was because the sons of Eli were backslidden and unbelieving; then his own children turn out the same way. This was the great prophet Samuel, who anointed David and confronted Saul, who decapitated Agag; the great Samuel, whose own children wound up the same way as the children of his mentor Eli. I get so much mail about this kind of situation, from people who have backslidden children and wonder whether God can still use them in spite of that. When your children are little and living at home, then the answer is no. However, once they grow up, they are no longer your responsibility. You will always love them, pray for them, support them, but you are no longer accountable for them. Can God use you despite the fact that your children may be rebellious, backslidden, and unbelieving? Well, not if they're little children, according to Timothy and Titus. But once they have grown up, don't let them hold you back; it didn't stop Samuel.

Next comes King David, who is the Old Testament shadow of Christ as the good shepherd as well as the king; he becomes the archetype of what a shepherd and a king should be like. In Kings and Chronicles David was always the plumbline – *"He walked before Me like his father David"* or *"He did not walk before Me like his father David"*, because David is a type of Christ. Jesus, Peter tells us, is the example of what a shepherd should be like. How good a pastor is your pastor? Well, how much like Jesus, the good shepherd, is he? For the Old Testament, David filled this role: how good a king was he, how good a shepherd? Well, how much like David was he? God took David and made him the standard, the type of Christ. David's second sin, numbering the people, was worse than his first. Yet look at his first sin – not on the worst day of your Christian life could you even begin to contrive what David actually did. He took a righteous man, Uriah – 'My light is Yahweh' – and set him up to be killed in order to take his wife. Uriah was loyal to God, to his country, and to David himself, yet David had him killed so that he could take his wife and conceal their adultery. Not on your worst day could you contemplate doing what David did. Even once he had done it, he failed to realise the seriousness of his sin. When the prophet Nathan came to him, his reaction was to shrug it off, as if he didn't even know he had done anything wrong. Yet this is the man who became the shadow of Christ? Wow – if there's hope for him, maybe there's even hope for me.

Scripture says *"For by faith the men of old gained approval"*–how could these sinful, depraved people gain approval? When you look at what they did, you must wonder how Hebrews can speak of them as it does. How could God forget what these people did? How could God pretend they had never acted as they had by the time the writer of Hebrews was inspired by the Holy Spirit to write as he did? How could God treat these people as if they had never done what they did and failed as they had? God can treat them as if they never did wrong for the same reason He can treat us as if we never did wrong. The reason God can treat them and us as if none of us did wrong is because He treated His own Son as if He had done it all. That is the gospel, and you have to be a total jerk to reject it. *"How shall we escape if we reject so great a salvation?"*

Hebrews holds these people up as our role models not because they didn't get it wrong or mess up, but precisely because they did. There's hope for them, therefore there's hope for us. Noah – ever meet a Christian who had a drinking problem? Abraham – ever tell a lie? Isaac – did you pass on your bad traits to your children? Sarah – did you ever doubt God? Joseph – have you ever faced rejection from the church and even from your family, been falsely accused and misunderstood, yet somehow found the grace to love them anyway? Moses, Rahab, Samson, Jephthah – look at what they did! What is God saying to us? If you have a sin problem you cannot conquer – and I can tell you that you certainly have one, though I couldn't tell you what it is – there is hope for you. Barak – if there's hope for that wimp, there's hope for any pathetic excuse for a head covering to which any of you women are married out there. Samuel – did you raise your children in the truth only to have them wander away, break your heart, and make a mess of their lives? *"Raise a child in the way he should go, and he will not forever depart from it."* May God prevent my children from falling away, but when children do fall away they normally come back. The question is how much of an unnecessary mess do they make of their lives and how much of an unnecessary grief do they cause before they do come back? And then there is David: this guy blew it big. There are also Christians who have blown it big. Yet if there is hope for these guys listed in Hebrews 11, there is hope, too, for us. Faith is the assurance of things hoped for; the **assurance**. People use 'hope' as a synonym for 'wish'; but faith is the assurance of what we hope for. I don't wish; I know there is hope for the hopeless.

One Messiah, Two Comings

And gathering them together, He commanded them not to leave Jerusalem, but to wait for what the Father had promised, "Which," He said, "You heard of from me; for John baptized with water, but you shall be baptised with the Holy Spirit not many days from now." And so when they had come together, they were asking Him, saying, "Lord, is it at this time You are restoring the kingdom to Israel?" He said to them, "It is not for you to know times or epochs which the Father has fixed by His own authority; but you shall receive power when the Holy Spirit has come upon you; and you shall be my witnesses both in Jerusalem, and in all Judea and Samaria, and even to the remotest part of the earth.'"

—Acts 1:4-8

Restorationism. "Lord, is it at this time You are restoring the kingdom?" We hear much talk today about a movement called the Restorationist Movement. The term "restoring the kingdom" is only used in one place in the New Testament, not in connection with the church triumphant, but with Israel. The Restoration Movement is committed to restoring three things which never existed to begin with. The first thing they are trying to restore is a version of eschatology, which is over-realised. It is called Dominionism or Triumphalism: the erroneous view that the church will conquer the world for Jesus, before He returns to set up His kingdom. The church will ultimately be victorious, but that victory depends on the return of Christ.And the God of peace will soon crush Satan under your feet (Roman 16:20). Daniel speaks specifically and plainly of the persecution that is to occur in the Last Days.

"I kept looking, and that horn [speaking of the Antichrist] was waging war with the saints and overpowering them until the Ancient of Days came, and judgment was passed in favour of the saints of the Highest One, and the time arrived when the saints took possession of the kingdom" (Daniel 7:21).

Kingdom Now theology falsely states that the saints will take possession of the kingdom before the return of Christ, but the Bible clearly teaches that they will take possession of the kingdom after the return of Christ. These kinds of erroneous beliefs have emerged at various times in church history, usually at turning points in world history.

During the decline of the Roman empire it was called Montanism. It exhibited much the same kind of chaos we see today with the modern Restoration Movement, including the emphasis on "signs and wonders" that drew people into it without any understanding of the biblical theology. Predictions, and prophecies that failed to happen, followed. During the Renaissance it was the Munster Anabaptists, who followed people called the Prophets of Zwickow — a group who did the same kind of things as the Kansas City Prophets do today, make wild and irresponsible predictions that fail to happen.

The second thing this movement is trying to restore is a view of prophetic authority which is not biblical. In the biblical version of prophetic authority, a prophet is responsible for what he says. I actually had somebody from the Vineyard tell me that the New Testament says that we "prophesy in part," so, therefore, John Wimber's followers, and Paul Cain, can be partly right and partly wrong, and still be biblical prophets. That idea is utterly false and terribly dangerous! People like that are deceived.

Thirdly, they are trying to restore a version of apostolic authority, which is not biblical. Apostolic authority in the New Testament was chiefly doctrinal. Does apostolic authority, in the sense of the twelve apostles, still exist in the church today? Yes it does. It exists in the writing of the apostles and of Paul. Apostolic authority was chiefly doctrinal and it exists today in the church, preserved by the Holy Spirit, in the writings of the apostles. Now there are other kinds of apostles, church-planting missionaries being among them, but as we look into the New Testament, apostolic authority was plural. *The Holy Spirit said, "Set apart for Me Barnabas and Saul for the work to which I have called them"* (Acts 13:2). Jesus sent the apostles out in pairs. Biblical authority was always plural.53 The model of apostolic authority in the House Church movement and in Restorationism is a pyramid scheme, where the apostle is the head honcho. What they are calling "apostolic authority" amounts to a form of heavy shepherding. Additionally, apostolic authority in the Bible is always accountable. Paul and Barnabas were always accountable back to Antioch, which sent them out. Beyond that, apostolic authority in the Bible involved *mutual submission* to each other, as in Acts chapter 15. It was never a one-man show. What they are calling "apostolic authority" today in the Restoration Movement is often only heavy shepherding, based on gnosticism. These people claim to have a gnosis, or a subjective revelation and, if you do not see it, they claim that you are under deception.

Nonetheless, there is a true restoration and that has to do with the restoration of Israel. Replacementism — the idea that the church has replaced Israel, to the negation of any prophetic or end times purpose for Israel and the Jews — is a totally unbiblical doctrine. Romans 11 speaks directly of Israel as "the root". The root supports you; you do not support the root. The root is under the ground. Just because you cannot see it, that does not mean that it is not there. If the tree had no root, the tree would die. If Israel was finished forever, the church would be finished with it. If God has rejected Israel because of their sin and unfaithfulness, He has just as much reason to reject the church, possibly more.

The sins of Israel are easily replayed throughout the history of the church, including the sacrifice of their children to demons, which we see today in the massive number of non-therapeutic abortions carried out even in Western, Christianised democracy. What Romans 11 teaches is that Gentile Christians who repent and accept Jesus, replace Jews who do not. They are grafted in as branches in place of Jews who reject their own Messiah, but the root remains Israel. Everything under the ground is Old Testament Israel, but everything above the ground is the New Testament church. The church is the spiritual continuity of Old Testament Israel, not its replacement. The root is still Jewish. The original branches were Jewish. The first Christians were Jews. The writers of the New Testament were Jews, and the final Christians will be Jews.

Jesus spoke of the national dimensions of the restoration of Israel in the Olivet Discourse — Jerusalem will be trampled under foot by the Gentiles until the time of the Gentiles be fulfilled (Luke 21:24). Jesus used the same words that Paul used in Romans 11:25, except that Jesus was speaking of Israel as a nation. The time of the Gentiles is dealt with soteriologically in Romans 11, but it is dealt with eschatologically in the Olivet Discourse in Luke 21.

The ultimate meaning of the time of the Gentiles coming to an end is bound up with the prophecies of Daniel. God's final plan for world redemption depends on the salvation of Israel and the fulfilment of His plan, prophetically, for the restoration of Israel. There is a national aspect of this but, more importantly, a soteriological, as seen in Romans 11:15. *"For if their rejection be the reconciliation of the world, what will their acceptance be but life from the dead?"*

The New Testament speaks of restoration, not in terms of this silly Triumphalist movement we have today, but in terms of God's plan for the restoration of Israel, through whom He will bless the nations. The Hebrew word for Gentile and the Hebrew word for nation is the same word, joy. God is going to bless the church through Jewish people in the last days. The Lord has given us these events in the Middle East as proof of the return of Christ. They are one of the signs Jesus has given.

Today we have many false teachers within the body of Christ who are misleading others, telling Christians that the very signs Jesus gave so the elect would not be unprepared or deceived, are not signs at all.

There are two main reasons why the Jewish people will reject Jesus as the Messiah. One is the unfortunate history of Christian anti-Semitism, usually carried out by the Roman Catholic church and the Eastern Orthodox church, but with the unfortunate exception of Martin Luther, whose works inspired Adolf Hitler in writing Mein Kampf. Luther taught that every Jew should be herded into a corral, forced to confess Christ at the point of knife. He said that "we, the German people, are to blame if we do not murder the Jews to prove we are Christians."

The second reason most Jews will reject Jesus as the Messiah is because Jesus did not bring in worldwide peace. He did not subdue the enemies of Israel, or establish the Messianic kingdom in Jerusalem, or bring justice to the nations, or prosperity and tranquillity to the world. If He is the Messiah, where is the Messianic reign in the character of David?

The answer is found in Daniel 9. The Messiah would have to come and die before the second temple would be destroyed. It was not the purpose of the Messiah to bring worldwide peace at His first coming. It was His purpose to deal with the source problem — sin. It will be at His second coming that He will bring in worldwide peace. *"And its end will come with flood and even to the end there will be war and desolations are determined"* (Daniel 9:26).

According to Judaism (the midrash Bereshith on page 243 of the Warsaw edition), the Messiah was to exit in 33AD. We read confirmation in the Talmudic literature also, confirming that the Messiah should have come and died before the second temple was destroyed. We read that the Sanhedrin wept and said, "Woe to us! Where is the Messiah? He had to have come by now."

Rabbi Leopold Cohen, a very senior, ultra-orthodox rabbi, sought to understand the meaning of Daniel chapter 9. He found two things in the Rabbinic literature of the ancient sages. One is that the Messiah was supposed to have come already. The other is that there is a curse on anybody who reads Daniel chapter 9. So Rabbi Leopold Cohen did the only honourable thing he could. He became a Baptist minister.

It's relatively easy to deal with the subject of Christian anti-Semitism. "How can you expect me to believe that Jesus is the Messiah when Christians murdered my grandparents?" The way you deal with the problem of Christian anti-Semitism is to tell Jewish people about the real Jesus — Jesus the Jew, Rabbi Yeshua Ben Yosef of Nazareth, and remind them that the Jewish people murdered their own prophets in the name of Moses. It was in the name of Moses that they put Jeremiah in prison, sawed Isaiah in half and killed Zechariah. Should you reject Moses because of what Jews did in his name? Should you reject Moses because of the orthodox Jew who recently went into a mosque in Hebron with an automatic weapon and murdered fifty Muslims? Do I blame Moses for that, because people murdered in his name? Well, then we cannot blame Jesus for what people have done over the centuries in His name. I have to accept Moses and the Torah on the basis of what Moses said. And I have to accept or reject Jesus and the New Testament on the basis of what He said and did.

The other subject though — why the Messiah did not bring in worldwide peace — is another issue. For Jesus to be the Messiah, He has to fulfil all the Messianic prophecies of the Old Testament. There are two kinds of Messianic prophecies in the Old Testament — the

MORE GRAIN FOR THE FAMINE

"Suffering Servant" prophecies (seen in the servant songs of Isaiah and elsewhere, and in some of the psalms of David), and also the "Davidic Messiah" of the conquering triumphal King who will subdue the enemies of God, establish the kingdom and bring in worldwide peace, reigning from Jerusalem. If Jesus is not the Messiah of the Jews, neither is He the Christ of the church. They mean the same thing: "Christ" and "Messiah," — the "Anointed One." Jesus has not fulfilled all of the Old Testament prophecies as yet. He has only fulfilled the "Son of David" prophecies in a spiritual sense, not yet in an historical sense. For Jesus to be the Messiah, He must fulfil all the prophecies.

The 'suffering servant' Messiah is called *HaMashiach Ben Yosef*, the Messiah, the Son of Joseph. The 'conquering king' Messiah is *HaMashiach Ben David*, the Messiah, the Son of David. We see this in the Jewish background of Palm Sunday.

Passover was one of three pilgrim feasts where the Jews sing something called the "Hallel Rabah" (from Psalms 113 to 118). The highlight of the Hallel Rabah is: *Hosanna, hosanna, blessed is He who comes in the name of the Lord. We bless you from the house of the Lord. Give thanks to the Lord, for He is good, for His loving kindness endures forever. Hosanna, hosanna.* The Jews were meant to sing that on Passover, with their hands waving. They were also meant to sing it at the Feast of Tabernacles, while waving palm branches in their hands.

On Palm Sunday, the Jews began to celebrate Passover (which teaches about the Messiah who was the Lamb who would be slain), as if it were the Feast of Tabernacles, which corresponds, in the typology of the Jewish calendar, to the millennium. The Feast of Tabernacles (seen in John 7:2), drawing on the background of Ezekiel 47, is associated in Jewish thought with the Davidic kingdom.That is why, when Jesus was transfigured with Moses and Elijah, Peter wanted to build three booths, three tabernacles. Peter was saying, "Here is the Messiah. Now let's set up the kingdom!"

When Jesus came on Palm Sunday, they wanted somebody who was going to get rid of the Romans, in the same way as the way the Maccabees had gotten rid of the Greeks, and set up the messianic kingdom. So they began to celebrate Passover, as if it were the Feast of Tabernacles.

In His first coming, Jesus fulfilled the first three (Spring) holidays in

54

the Jewish calendar: Passover, First Fruits (which was the resurrection), and the Feast of Weeks (which was Pentecost).

In His second coming, Jesus will fulfil the last three (Autumn) holidays: the Feast of Trumpets, the Day of Atonement, and finally and ultimately, the Feast of Tabernacles.

The Jews of His day did not want to know about a suffering servant Messiah, who was going to come as the Passover Lamb to be slain. They wanted a conquering king, who was going to set up the millennium.

The suffering servant Messiah is called "the Son of Joseph," *HaMashiach Ben Yosef*. The conquering king Messiah is called "the Son of David," *HaMashiach Ben David*. For Jesus of Nazareth to be the Messiah, He has to fulfil ALL the prophecies. But Jesus has plainly and clearly not fulfilled all the prophecies. He has only fulfilled the suffering servant ones, the Son of Joseph ones. In other words, it is one Messiah, two comings.

In His first coming Jesus came as the Son of Joseph, the suffering servant. In His second coming He will return as the Son of David, the conquering king who will set up His kingdom.

The doctrines of Amillennialism and Postmillennialism were the invention of the Roman Catholic Church, following the errors of Constantine and Augustine, at the time when Christendom was made the religion of the state. Amillennialism and Post Millennialism are totally unbiblical.

From the original Jewish perspective of the New Testament, only a Premillennial position is tenable. If there is no millennium, Jesus is not the Messiah. And, if He is not the Messiah for the Jews, neither is He the Christ for the church. He must fulfil all the Old Testament prophecies and, so far, He has only fulfilled the Son of Joseph prophecies.

What the apostles were really asking with the question, "Lord, is it at this time you are restoring the kingdom?" was: "We know that you are the son of Joseph, but when are you going to be the son of David? When are you going to restore the kingdom the way David did?"

Even John the Baptist could not understand this. *"And summoning two of his disciples, John sent them to the Lord, saying, 'Are You the expected one, or do we look for someone else?'"* (Luke 7:19).

Even the apostles, after the resurrection, on the Mount of Olives at the ascension, were unable to understand that it is one Messiah, but two comings. In His first coming, the Lord Jesus was the Messiah, the Son of Joseph. In His second coming, He will be the Messiah, the Son of David, the conquering king who will fully establish the kingdom.

Let us look at Jesus, the son of Joseph.

Beloved of his father

"Now Israel loved Joseph more than all of his sons" (Genesis 37:3). Joseph was the beloved son of his father.

"And behold, a voice out of the heavens, saying, 'This is My beloved Son, in whom I am well pleased'" (Matthew 3:17). The Messiah, the son of Joseph, was the beloved son of His Father.

Fellowship and service

"Then he [Jacob] said to him [Joseph], 'Go now and see about the welfare of your brothers and the welfare of the flock; and bring word back to me.' So he sent him from the valley of Hebron, and he came to Shechem" (Genesis 37:14). Joseph lived in Hebron which, in Hebrew, means "the place of fellowship." Joseph dwelt with His father at the place of fellowship and was sent by his father to seek the welfare of his brothers.

"Have this attitude in yourselves which was also in Christ Jesus, who, although He existed in the form of God, did not regard equality with God a thing to be grasped, but emptied Himself , taking the form of a bondservant, and being made in the likeness of men" (Philippians 2:5-7).

"For God so loved the world that He gave His only begotten Son that whoever believes in Him should not perish but have eternal life" (John 3:16).

Jesus dwelt with His Father in the place of fellowship and was sent by His Father to seek the welfare of His brothers.

His brothers' sins

"And Joseph brought back a bad report about them to his father" (Genesis 37:2). Joseph testified to his father about the sins of his brothers, and his brothers hated him.

"If the world hates you, you know that it has hated Me before it hated you. If you were of the world, the world would love its own; but because you are not of the world, but I chose you out of the world, therefore the world hates you" (John 15:18-19). Jesus testified about the sins of His brothers and so they hated Him.

They hated him still more

"Then Joseph had a dream, and when he told it to his brothers, they hated him even more" (Genesis 37:5). Joseph revealed to his brothers the exalted position he was to receive. They already hated him for testifying against their sins, but now they absolutely despised him.

"And then the sign of the Son of Man will appear in the sky, and then all the tribes of the earth will mourn, and they will see the Son of Man coming on the clouds in the sky with power and great glory" (Matthew 24:30).

"And the scribes and chief priests tried to lay hands on him that very hour, and they feared the people; for they understood that he spoke this parable against them" (Luke 20:19). Jesus revealed to His brothers the position of glory that He would receive and so His brothers hated Him.

Foretold that he would rule

Joseph told his brothers that *"we were binding sheaves in the field, and lo, my sheaf rose up and also stood erect; and behold, your sheaves gathered around and bowed down to my sheaf"* (Genesis 37:7).

"You shall see the Son of Man sitting at the right hand of Power" (Matthew 26:64). Joseph foretold that one day he would rule. Jesus foretold that one day He would rule.

Rejected and condemned

"When they saw him from a distance and before he came close to them, they plotted against him to put him to death" (Genesis 37:18).

"We do not want this man to reign over us" (Luke 19:14).

"But they kept on crying out, saying, 'Crucify, crucify Him!'" (Luke 23:21). Both were rejected and condemned to die.

Out of His mind

"And they said to one another, 'Here comes this dreamer!'" (Gen. 37:19).

"And when His own people heard of this, they went to take custody of Him; for they were saying, 'He has lost His senses'" (Mark 3:21).

Joseph was accused by his brothers of being a dreamer. They said of Jesus, the Messiah, the son of Joseph, that He had lost His senses.

Sold for silver

"And Judah said to his brothers, 'What prof it is it for us to kill our brother and cover up his blood? Come and let us sell him to the Ishmaelites and not lay our hands on him; for he is our brother, our own flesh.' And his brothers listened to him.

Then some Midianite traders passed by, so they pulled him up and lifted Joseph out of the pit, and sold him to the Ishmaelites for twenty shekels of silver" (Genesis 37:26-28).

Judah betrayed Joseph and sold him for twenty pieces of silver.

"Then one of the twelve, named Judas Iscariot, went to the chief priests, and said, 'What are you willing to give me to deliver Him to you?' And they weighed out for him thirty pieces of silver" (Matthew 26:151). Judah betrayed Joseph for twenty pieces of silver. Judas (same name as "Judah" in Hebrew) betrayed the son of Joseph, after inflation, for thirty pieces of silver.

Servant's heart

"So Joseph found favour in his sight, and he became his personal servant; and he made him overseer over his house, and all that he owned he put in his charge" (Genesis 39:4). Everything Joseph did, he did as a servant.

Luke 22:25-27 and Philippians 2:7 tell us that everything Jesus did, He did as a servant.

Everything to prosper

"And it came about that from the time he made him overseer in his house, and over all that he owned, the Lord blessed the Egyptian's house on account of Joseph" (Genesis 39:5). The Lord caused all that Joseph did to prosper.

"And the good pleasure of the Lord will prosper in his hand" (Isaiah 53:10). God shall cause all that the son of Joseph does to prosper.

Tempted

"And it came about after these events that his master's wife looked with desire at Joseph, and she said, 'Lie with me'. But he refused and said to his master's wife, 'Behold, with me here, my master does not concern himself with anything in the house, and he has put all that he owns in my charge. There is no one greater in this house than I, and he has withheld nothing from me except you, because you are his wife. How then could I do this great evil, and sin against God?'" (Gen. 39:7-9). Joseph was tempted to the utmost, but he endured and would not sin.

"Then Jesus was led by the Spirit into the wilderness to be tempted by the devil... Then Jesus said to him, 'Begone, Satan! For it is written, You shall worship the Lord your God, and serve Him only.' Then the devil left Him..." (Matthew 4:1-11). Joseph was tempted to the utmost and endured. The Messiah, the son of Joseph, was tempted to the utmost, but He endured.

Falsely accused

"When she saw that he had left his garment in her hand, and had fled outside, she called to the men of her household, and said to them, 'See, he has brought in a Hebrew to make sport of us; he came in to me to lie with me, and I screamed. And it came about when he heard that I raised my voice and screamed, that he left his garment beside me and fled, and went outside'" (Genesis 39:13-15). Joseph was falsely accused.

"Now, the chief priests and the whole Council kept trying to obtain false testimony against Jesus, in order that they might put Him to death; and they did not find any, even though many false witnesses came forward. But later on two came forward and said, "This man stated, 'I am able to destroy the temple of God and rebuild it in three days.'" And the high priest stood up and said to Him, "Do You make no answer? What is this that these men are testifying against You?" But Jesus kept silent. And the high priest said to Him, "I adjure you by the living God, that You tell us whether You are the Messiah, the Son of God." Jesus said, "You have said it yourself ; nevertheless I tell you, hereafter you shall see the Son of Man sitting at the right hand of Power, and coming on the clouds of heaven." Then the high priest tore his robes, saying, "He has blasphemed! What further need do we have of witnesses? Behold, you have now heard the blasphemy…" (Matthew 26:59- 65). Joseph was accused falsely and lied about. The Messiah, the son of Joseph, was accused falsely and lied about.

Predicted life and death

"Then the cupbearer and the baker for the king of Egypt, who were confined in jail, both had a dream the same night, each man with his own dream and each dream with its own interpretation … Then Joseph said to [the cupbearer], "This is the interpretation of it: the three branches are three days; within three more days Pharaoh will lift up your head and restore you to your off ice; and you will put Pharaoh's cup into his hand according to your former custom when you were his cupbearer … Then Joseph answered and said [to the baker], "This is its interpretation: the three baskets are three days; within three more days Pharaoh will lift up your head from you and hang you on a tree; and the birds will eat your flesh off you" (Genesis 40:5-19).

Joseph predicted that one of these criminals would live and that the other one would die. *"And one of the criminals who were hanging there was hurling abuse at Him, saying, 'Are You not the Christ? Save Yourself and us!' But the other answered, and rebuking him said, 'Do you not even fear God, since you are under the same sentence of condemnation? And we indeed justly, for we are receiving what we deserve for our deeds; but this man has done nothing wrong.' And he was saying, 'Jesus, remember me when You come in your kingdom!' And He said to him, 'Truly I say to you, today you shall be with Me in Paradise'"* (Luke 23:39-43). Jesus was condemned with two criminals and, as He predicted, one lived and one died.

Promised deliverance
"Then Joseph said to him, 'This is the interpretation of it: the three branches are three days; within three more days Pharaoh will lift up your head and restore you to your office; and you will put Pharaoh's cup into his hand according to your former custom when you were his cupbearer'" (Genesis 40:12-13). Joseph promised deliverance to a condemned man.

"And he was saying, 'Jesus, remember me when You come in Your kingdom!'And Jesus said to him, 'Truly I say to you, today you shall be with Me in Paradise'" (Luke 23:42-43). Yeshua, the son of Joseph promised deliverance to a condemned man. And that same son of Joseph is promising deliverance to condemned men today if they will repent and ask Him to forgive them, and follow Him.

A way of salvation
Joseph was betrayed by his Jewish brothers into the hands of Gentiles, but God took this betrayal and turned it around and made it a way for all of Israel, and all of the world, to be saved. So too, the Messiah, the son of Joseph, was betrayed by His Jewish brothers into the hands of Gentiles. God took this betrayal and turned it around, making it a way for all Israel, and all the world, to be saved.

Forgotten by those he helped *"Yet the chief cupbearer did not remember Joseph, but forgot him"* (Genesis 40:23). *And Jesus answered and said, "Were there not ten cleansed? But the nine — where are they? Was no one found who turned back to give glory to God, except this foreigner?"* (Luke 17:17,18). Joseph was forgotten by those he helped, and the son of Joseph was forgotten by those He helped.
Raised to glory
"Then Pharaoh sent and called for Joseph, and they hurriedly brought him out of the dungeon; and when he had shaved himself and changed his clothes, he came to Pharaoh. So Pharaoh said to Joseph, 'Since God has informed you of all this, there is no one so discerning and wise as you are. You shall be over my house, and according to your command all my people shall do homage; only in the throne I will

be greater than you'" (Genesis 41:14,39- 40). Joseph was taken from a dungeon, a place of death, and he was raised by the king to the place of glory in one day.

"I pray that the eyes of your heart may be enlightened, so that you may know what is the hope of His calling, what are the riches of the glory of His inheritance in the saints, and what is the surpassing greatness of His power towards us who believe. These are in accordance with the working of the strength of His might which He brought about in Christ, when He raised Him from the dead, and seated Him at His right hand in the heavenly places, far above all rule and authority and power and dominion, and every name that is named, not only in this age, but also in the one to come" (Ephesians 1:19-20). Joseph was raised from a place of condemnation to a place of glory in one day, and the son of Joseph, the Messiah, the Lord Jesus, was raised from a place of condemnation to a place of glory in a single day.

Wonderful counsellor

"So Pharaoh said to Joseph, 'Since God has informed you of all this, there is no one so discerning and wise as you are'" (Genesis 41:39). Joseph proved to be a great counsellor. In Isaiah 9:6 we read that *"And His name will be called Wonderful Counsellor."*

Highly exalted

"And Pharaoh said to Joseph, 'See I have set you over all the land of Egypt'" (Genesis 41:41). Joseph was promoted to glory and honour and given a new name.

"Therefore also God highly exalted Him, and bestowed on Him the name which is above every name" (Phil. 2:9). Jesus was promoted to glory and honour and given a new name.

Took a Gentile bride

"Then Pharaoh named Joseph Zaphenath-Paneah; and he gave him Asenath, the daughter of Potiphera priest of On, as his wife. And Joseph went forth over the land of Egypt" (Genesis 41:45). After being exalted, Joseph took a Gentile bride.

"For the husband is the head of the wife, as Christ also is the head of the church, He Himself being the Saviour of the Body" (Ephesians 5:23-32). Jesus, after exaltation, took a Gentile bride — in figure, the Gentile church. That is why the book of Ruth — the story of a Jewish man

taking a Gentile bride — is read in the synagogues at Pentecost, which we call "the birthday of the church." And, in both cases, the brides were given to share the glory.

About thirty years of age

"Now Joseph was thirty years old when he stood before Pharaoh, king of Egypt." (Genesis 41:46). Joseph was 30 years old when he began his work.

"And when He began His ministry, Jesus Himself was about thirty years of age... " (Luke 3:23). The son of Joseph was 30 years old when He began His work.

"Do whatever He says"

"So when all the land of Egypt was famished, the people cried out to Pharaoh for bread; and Pharaoh said to all the Egyptians, 'Go to Joseph; whatever he says to you, you shall do'" (Genesis 41:55).

"His (Jesus') mother said to the servants, 'Whatever He says to you, do it'" (John 2:5). Of Joseph it was said *"Do whatever he tells you"*. Of the son of Joseph it was said, *"Do whatever He tells you"*.

Every knee shall bow

"Then Pharaoh took off his signet ring from his hand, and put it on Joseph's hand, and clothed him in garments of fine linen, and put the gold necklace around his neck. And he had him ride in his second chariot; and they proclaimed before him, 'Bow the knee!' And he set him over all the land of Egypt. Moreover, Pharaoh said to Joseph, 'Though I am Pharaoh, yet without your permission no one shall raise his hand or foot in all the land of Egypt'" (Genesis 41:42-44). When he was exalted, every knee bowed to Joseph and he was given all power and glory.

"Therefore also God highly exalted Him, and bestowed on Him the name which is above every name, that at the name of Jesus every knee should bow, of those who are in heaven, and on earth, and under the earth, and that every tongue should confess that Jesus Christ is Lord, to the glory of God the Father" (Philippians 2:9-11). *"And Jesus came up and spoke to them, saying, 'All authority has been given to me in heaven and on earth'"* (Matthew 28:18). Every knee shall bow to the Son of Joseph, and He has been given all power and glory.

The Bread of Life

"So when all the land of Egypt was famished, the people cried out to Pharaoh for bread; and Pharaoh said to all the Egyptians, 'Go to Joseph; whatever he says to you, you shall do.' When the famine was spread over all the face of the earth, then Joseph opened all the storehouses, and sold to the Egyptians; and the famine was severe in the land of Egypt, And the people of all the earth came to Egypt to buy grain from Joseph, because the famine was severe in the earth" (Genesis 41:55-57).

"Jesus said to them, 'I am the bread of life; he who comes to Me shall not hunger, and he who believes in Me shall never thirst'" (John 6:35). *"And there is salvation in no one else; for there is no other name under heaven that has been given among men, by which we must be saved"* (Acts 4:12). The whole world had to get their bread from Joseph — there was no other way the people could be saved. And there is no way for us to be saved except through the son of Joseph.

Not entrusting Himself to men

"Now they were seated before him, the firstborn according to his birthright and the youngest according to his youth, and the men looked at one another in astonishment" (Gen. 43:33). Why? Because Joseph knew the past sinful history of his brothers.

"But Jesus, on His part, was not entrusting Himself to them, for He knew all men, and because He did not need anyone to bear witness concerning man for He Himself knew what was in man" (John 2:24,25). Jesus the Messiah is like Joseph, knowing the past history and sins of his brothers.

Not recognised first time

However, as we read in Genesis, Joseph's brothers do not recognise him at the first coming. They recognised him at the second. *"Joseph could not control himself before all those who stood by him, and he cried, 'Have everyone go out from me'. So there was no man with him when Joseph made himself known to his brothers. And he wept so loudly that the Egyptians heard it, and the household of Pharaoh heard of it. Then Joseph said to his brothers, 'I am Joseph! Is my father still alive?' But his brothers could not answer him, for they were dismayed at his presence. Then Joseph said to his brothers, 'Please come closer to me'. So they came closer. And he said, 'I am your brother Joseph, whom you sold into Egypt'"* (Genesis 45:1-4). Joseph's brothers did not recognise him at the first coming, but at the second.

"And I will pour out on the house of David and on the inhabitants of Jerusalem, the Spirit of grace and of supplication, so they will look upon Me who they have pierced; and they will mourn for Him, as one mourns for an only son, and they will weep bitterly over Him, like the bitter weeping over a first born" (Zechariah 12:10). The brothers of the Messiah, the son of Joseph, did not recognise him at his first coming, but they will at the second, realising the one they betrayed is now the exalted one who was going to save them. The one who was crucified is the one who is the redeemer, the king.

The son of Joseph is also the son of David. The suffering servant is also the conquering king. When his brothers repented, he forgave them. And when Jesus' brothers, the Jewish people repent, He forgives them. In the beginning Joseph used the Egyptian people, the Gentiles, to give bread to his brothers, but a time came when the Gentiles were sent away and he revealed himself to his brothers. Right now the son of Joseph is using Gentiles, Christians, to send the food, the Bread of Life, to His brothers, but a time will come in the great tribulation when the son of Joseph will personally reveal Himself to His brothers.

All power to the King

"Joseph, after his exaltation, turned around and delivered all into the hands of Pharaoh" (Genesis 47:20).

"Then comes the end, when He delivers up the kingdom to the God and Father, when He has abolished all rule and authority and power" (1 Corinthians 15:24). Joseph gave all rule and authority and power into the hands of the king. The Messiah, the son of Joseph, will give all power and rule into the hands of the king.

Saviour

"So they said, 'You have saved our lives! Let us find favour in the sight of my lord, and we will be Pharoah's slaves'" (Genesis 47:25). Joseph was acknowledged to be the people's saviour.

"For the grace of God has appeared, bringing salvation to all men, instructing us to deny ungodliness and worldly desires and to live sensibly, righteously and godly in the present age, looking for the blessed hope and the appearing of the glory of our great God and Saviour., Christ Jesus; who gave Himself for us, that He might redeem us from every lawless deed and purify for Himself a people for His own possession, zealous for good deeds" (Titus 2:11-14). The Messiah, the son of

Joseph, the Lord Jesus Christ, is acknowledged to be the Saviour of all mankind.

Not recognised

When Joseph was adorned (Genesis 41:42) with the garments of Egyptian royalty, he became totally unrecognisable to his Hebrew brothers (Genesis 42:8). After the first century, Jesus was taken and made king of the Gentiles. It was forgotten that He came as King of the Jews and He became totally unrecognisable to His Hebrew brothers. One Messiah: Two Comings.

Joseph was given a new name upon his exaltation (Genesis 41:45). The Gentiles call Rabbi Yeshua Ben Yosef by a new name — Jesus — a Greek name, not His original one. One Messiah, two comings.

The Jews did not recognise Joseph at the first coming but at the second. And they will recognise the son of Joseph at the second coming, seeing the one who was betrayed and crucified as the one who has indeed come to bring salvation. One Messiah, two comings.

Jesus is coming back as the son of David. Every eye will see Him. The Jews will look upon Him whom they have pierced and mourn as one mourns for an only son. Those who look upon Jesus, whom we have all pierced, and mourn now as one mourns for an only son, will have the same blessing and promise that He gives to His own people. The Messiah, the son of Joseph, will return as the Messiah, the son of David. And He will restore the kingdom to Israel.

Divine Aristocracy

L et us look at a few verses in Proverbs before turning to our main text in Ecclesiastes. Proverbs 8:6-11: *"Listen, for I shall speak noble things, and the opening of my lips will produce right things. My mouth will utter truth; wickedness is an abomination to my lips. All of the utterances of my mouth are in righteousness; there is nothing crooked or perverted in them. They are all straightforward to him who understands, and right to those who find knowledge. Take my instruction, not silver, and knowledge rather than choice gold; for wisdom is better than jewels, and all desirable things cannot compare with her."*

Instruction from God, we are told, is better than silver. Knowledge of Him and of His Word is better than gold, and wisdom is better than jewels.

The world has its aristocracy; they will always look for gold, silver, jewels, annuities, investment portfolios, securities, etc. The world will look to material wealth – its aristocracy must and will have all of these things that will not matter in eternity. God says, however, that only the things that last forever are real riches. Silver, gold and jewels will not get you off the road to hell – nor will they get you into heavenly Jerusalem.

There are two aspects to this: First, we often forget that "the meek shall inherit the earth": there will be a literal millennial reign of Jesus. When that time comes, God's aristocracy will rule and reign with Christ on this planet. Then there is the second aspect, which is eternity.

One way to understand this is as follows: there are certain things in life and in scripture that teach us now about the millennium. For example, antediluvian man lived to be hundreds of years old, and that teaches how it will be again in the millennium. Other experiences such as the love you feel for a beautiful newborn baby, or the thrill of looking on an unblemished landscape where pollution has not disturbed the natural environment – the best things in this life can give us a dim view of what the millennium will be like; it will be what would have happened on this planet if Adam and Eve had not sinned. In turn, the millennium will be used by God to teach us what heaven will be like. When Jesus reigns in Jerusalem, He will personally teach us the things of the Father. The meek will inherit the earth: God's aristocracy will take over this planet. The Jehovah's Witnesses completely corrupt this, but it is nonetheless a biblical truth.

Then there is eternity, to which the only treasures we may bring are knowledge, wisdom, and understanding. The world can and does have data; however, there is a big difference between data and knowledge. There are people who have degrees in theology from the finest universities, who know all about the Bible; yet they have no idea what the Bible is about. They have data, but no knowledge. To gain knowledge one needs understanding. One may have data, but to know what the data means requires understanding, and gaining understanding, in turn, requires wisdom. The world has its folly, which it calls wisdom, but it totally lacks true wisdom.

God's aristocracy has something better than gold, silver, and jewels. The world will always measure wealth by the things that perish, while God measures wealth by eternal, imperishable things. However, just as the world measures wealth by material riches, so also do worldly churches. The standard of a worldly church is the same as that used by the world.

We have an example of this in what Jesus said to the church of Laodicea: *"You say you are rich, that you have need of nothing; not knowing that you are wretched, pitiable, poor, blind and naked"* (Rev 3:17). The general superintendent of the Assemblies of God in Australia wrote a book called *You Need More Money*, in which he claims that the fact that God has blessed his ministry financially proves him to be in good favour and standing with Him, while those who disapprove of his ministry are not blessed with material wealth and are therefore out of God's will. That is a classic example of someone using the world's standard to judge the things and the people of God. Jesus, however, tells the church of Laodicea that they, who think they are rich, are the ones who are truly impoverished. Remember: Laodicea's first problem is that it doesn't know it is Laodicea. Jesus tells them to *"buy salve to anoint your eyes, that you may see*" (Rev 3:18). Suburban middle-class Protestantism does not know that it's not ready for Jesus to come back. It is the faithful remnant in Laodicea who know, and who buy eye salve.

Why do faithful Christians so often struggle more than worldly believers? Why do good Christians so often have more trials than do worldly Christians? Why do good, biblical churches so often struggle more than worldly churches? Because it is those whom He loves that God corrects. The others become, as it were, illegitimate children.

So we see from scripture that Laodicea measures wealth in the same way the world does; but how does Jesus measure wealth? He tells Laodicea "You have the wealth, but you're impoverished," yet He tells the church in Smyrna this in Rev. 2:9: *"I know your tribulation and your poverty, but you are rich"*. The name 'Smyrna' is derived from the Greek word for myrrh, which was used to anoint dead bodies for burial in the ancient world. Remember that Jesus was buried with a mixture of aloes and myrrh; myrrh has to do with death. The Magi brought very significant gifts to Jesus: gold because He would be King, frankincense because He would be Priest, but then myrrh because He would die, would be a Sacrifice anointed for burial.

Which are the truly rich churches today? The rich churches are those that do not hope in this world: Christians in persecuted churches belong to the true divine aristocracy. I am not saying you must be persecuted in order to be in the aristocracy, but you must be *willing* to be persecuted, and if necessary, to give up material, financial position and security for the cause of the gospel of Christ. God has His aristocracy: those who have wisdom, knowledge and understanding. These are the riches of His nobility. (The Hebrew word for aristocracy and nobility is the same.)

With this background in view, please turn to Ecclesiastes 9. You may have heard me point out that just as Proverbs is God's psychology book, so Ecclesiastes is God's philosophy text. The Greeks had Aristotle, Plato, and Socrates; the Germans had the 19th-century rationalists like Nietzsche and Hegel; the English had Hobbes and Beetham. In Hebrew Ecclesiastes is called *kohelet*, the Preacher. God's philosophy is simply this: This world is fallen, and it is futile to put trust in it; it is all vanity. If you trust it, you'll be very disappointed. Fear God and keep His commandments, trusting Him for something much better. This place is fallen.

God's philosophy stated in brief actually says, "Make the best of a bad thing". It tells people to make the most of their youth, to make the most of their marriage, because these things are fleeting; it tells us to fear God and keep His commandments rather than put any trust in the things that are temporal. If trust is placed in this world, it leads to bitter disappointment at the very least. That is God's philosophy.

> "For I have taken all this into my heart to explain it, that righteous men and wise men and their deeds are in God's hand. Man does not know whether it will be love or hatred; anything awaits him. It is the same for all: There is one fate for the righteous and one for the wicked, for the good and for the clean, and for the unclean, for the man who offers a sacrifice and for the one who does not offer a sacrifice. As the good man is, so is the sinner. As the swearer is, so is the one who is afraid to swear" (Ecclesiastes 9:1).

In the New Testament, James tells us in his epistle not to boast about tomorrow, but to say "if the Lord wills". This is particularly or acutely true of salvation – *"now is the appointed time, today is the day of salvation"*. You do not know what is on the agenda; nobody knows but the Lord Himself. Yet we do know that because the world is fallen, something has happened: good people and bad people both die. The rich and the poor go to the same grave. The good people – that is, those who are justified by faith in Christ – will have the hope of the resurrection.

However, the fact is that the rich man cannot take his wealth with him; it ends with his death. It makes no difference how high and mighty a person is: once he dies, it's all over. Once Princess Diana died, she was in exactly the same situation as the next person who may have been totally unknown in his lifetime here.

Our office in England is near the castle of George Harrison of the Beatles – we tried to witness to him a few times and gave him the book *Death of a Guru*, but it was difficult to even get him to hear us because he was so steeped in Hinduism. He died chanting Hare Krishna in Los Angeles, the newspapers tell us. Well, his castle is no longer his; he did not take it with him to Nirvana. As far as we can know, he took nothing with him into hell. It is the same for all mankind in the end.

Continuing in Ecclesiastes 9:3 –

"This is an evil in all that is done under the sun: that one thing happens to all. Truly the hearts of the sons of men are full of evil; madness is in their hearts while they live, and after that they go to the dead."

God sees the fact that both good and bad people end up dead as an evil. *"The whole world lies in the power of the wicked one"*; expect no enduring justice in this world. God can and will intervene for His purposes on behalf of His people, but don't expect much from this place. Continuing in verse 4:

"But for him who is joined to all the living there is hope, for a living dog is better than a dead lion."

The reference for this would be II Samuel 9:8. The most miserable, downcast born-again Christian is infinitely better off than the most successful, together unsaved person. The most depressed, basket-case excuse for a Christian is still infinitely better off than an unsaved person who has got it all together, no matter how big their investment portfolio is or how much property they own or how professionally successful they are. A sick dog is always better than a dead lion; unsaved people are dead. Ecclesiastes 9:5 –

"For the living know that they will die; but the dead know nothing, and they have no more reward, for the memory of them is forgotten."

The only reward that an unsaved person will receive is what they can get out of this world, which will be over before they know it.

What does it mean that the dead know nothing? It is amazing to me how many Christians ask me what happens when we die. Studying the subject of death in the Bible is called *thanatology*, from the Greek word *thanos*. We're thinking of doing a conference on this subject. When you die, will you go to be with the Lord, or will you go to sleep? Well, time as we know it exists only relative to us. In eternity, there is *chronos*, from which we get the word 'chronology'; it means an order of events outside time. What most of us are inclined to do is to think of eternity as a clock that keeps going forever. We translate the Greek term *kairos* and the Hebrew term *olama olamin* as 'forever and ever', but their meaning is not exactly that, although it does include that. It is not a clock that continues 'forever and ever', but rather the absence of any clock at all.

The Bible talks about the deaths of Christians as sleep for two reasons: First, when you go to sleep, you wake up again. The next thing a person knows after they have fallen asleep is that they are waking up, just as Christians who have died or 'fallen asleep' before Christ comes will arise at the resurrection having been unaware of the time that passed between their earthly death and the resurrection event. Relative to us, relative to time, those who have died in Christ are asleep and awaiting the resurrection. They are unconscious of anything that is going on in this world, although believers who die are in the conscious presence of the Lord in eternity (we must not confuse this truth with the error of "soul sleep").

The second reason the Bible uses the illustration of sleep is this: a person's consciousness enters a different realm while they sleep. Neurophysiologists tell us that everybody dreams. They derive this information from observing brain wave activity, eyes flickering, etc. In a dream, it is possible to talk to and be with people who are dead as if they are alive again, and it makes sense in the context of the dream. It is possible to see past events happening in the present. It is also possible to dream of future events which have not yet happened. Somehow, the past, present, and future can all be the same in a dream. You have chronos, a chronology of events, but no time.

Think of what happens to John in the book of Revelation: he enters eternity and sees the 24 elders in Revelation 4, who are the 12 patriarchs of Israel and the 12 apostles; he, of course, is one of these apostles and elders, and so sees himself in eternity. Another example from scripture is that the Lamb was slain from before the foundation of the world; outside of time. Scripture tells us that we are already seated with Christ in the heavenly places – part of our problem is that we do not see ourselves from an eternal perspective, the way Ephesians describes it. We are already the aristocracy. When we die, we enter eternity, which is a different realm. Therefore, relative to the one who dies, he is with the Lord. But relative to this realm, this earth, the next thing that one will be aware of is the resurrection.

Part of the problem with Calvinism is that they try to apply time to eternity. Because Calvinism is based on humanism, Calvinists try to figure things out intellectually which can only be comprehended intellectually to a certain point. They like to emphasise that we're predestined – well, of course, because relative to eternity every choice has already been made. Do I believe in eternal security? Yes, because we are already seated with Christ in heavenly places; in eternity it's already happening. I believe in eternal security as the Bible teaches it. But once saved always saved? No – relative to us it is a variable. Again, this is a thing we can only understand to a certain point.

In England we call American football 'gridiron'; it's not so popular, though some people like it. I, however, prefer a game called rugby. So when I have to speak at a church and there's a rugby match on, I try to get someone to videotape it for me. (I do NOT like it when people tell me the scores, which has happened to me twice.) Then, when I get home, I watch the match. Relative to the players, the match is a done deal; it's over. I, however, can be just as involved in the game after the fact (as long as nobody tells me something they shouldn't) as if I were watching it in real time. Relative to me, the match is still going on and can go either way. Our relationship to time and eternity is something like that; to try explaining it any further is beyond me – that is the most the Bible tells us.

"The dead know nothing"; they are asleep. When people are asleep or comatose, they are unaware of the events around them, but that is not to say that they don't have any consciousness: their consciousness has simply entered a different realm. Those, then, are the two reasons the Bible uses sleep as an illustration of what death is like for believers.

Continued in Ecclesiastes 9 verse 5b:

> "For the memory of them is forgotten. Also their love, their hatred, and their envy have now perished; nevermore shall they have a share in anything done under the sun."

So once you leave this place, it's a done deal. Verse 7:

> "Go, eat your bread with joy, and drink your wine with a merry heart; for God has already accepted your works."

Jesus said that He had meat to eat which was to do the will of the Father. Ecclesiastes is drawing there on pascal imagery, the fulfilment of which is found in the Lord's Supper, by which we proclaim the Lord's death until He comes. When we take the Lord's supper, we're remembering what Jesus did for us. It is an appetiser before the marriage supper of the Lamb; although the world is perishing, we can eat the bread and drink the cup with gladness, because we know where we came from – the cross and the empty tomb – and we know where we're going – heaven. Therefore we can eat and drink with a glad heart. The Lord's Supper should really be the centerpiece of our fellowship and worship. Fellowship is important, worship is important, exposition of the scripture is important – it is all important, but the centerpiece and the highlight should be the breaking of bread. We proclaim His death until He comes; it's where we came from and it's where we're going. It is a memorial, but it is also a prelude to the marriage supper.

"For God has already accepted your works" – look, please, at II Timothy 1:9: *"(God) who has saved us and called us with a holy calling, not according to our works, but according to His own purpose and grace which was given to us in Christ Jesus from all eternity"*. Now, you know that in the Bible when it says "Christ Jesus", with the Messianic title preceding His personal name, it speaks of Him in eternity. When it says "Jesus Christ", personal name first and Messianic title second, it refers to Him on earth. God has saved us and called us: there is a difference between salvation and calling.

What the New Testament really says about election has more to do with our calling than with our salvation. Just as we are already saved from eternity – to us it's a variable, but to eternity it's completed – so our works, the ministry to which God has called us, was also ordained from eternity. Before you were born, before you were born again, before the planet was even created, God ordained what He had for you to do.

Now, according to Matthew 25, the magnitude of our eternal reward will depend in large measure upon whether or not we are faithful to God's calling. "God has already approved your works' – why? Because they were ordained from eternity; it has already happened. If you have the gift of evangelism, that was ordained from eternity; if you have the gift of a pastor, that was ordained from eternity. The same goes for music ministry, the gift of helps, the gift of teaching, or God's calling of a person to a third-world country as a missionary. *"Eat your bread with joy and drink your wine with gladness"* – take the Lord's supper with joy, because what you are doing God has already approved from eternity.

It is God's philosophy that we must see things from the eternal perspective, as Ephesians states. That is one of the barometers of spiritual growth: the older you get in Jesus, the more you should view your life from the perspective of eternity. Unsaved people have nothing to live for but fear of the grave, so they become obsessed with this life and this world. We know that God has already approved our works; so if there's a believer who by the will of the Lord is in prison for his faith, God has already approved that he will be there as a witness to his faith. He can still eat his bread and drink his wine with gladness in spite of his circumstances in this life, for he knows where he is going. We see this in Paul – when he was in prison, he knew that he was in the will of God and so rejoiced.

Let's continue in Ecclesiastes 9:8–

"Let your garments always be white, and let your head lack no oil."

The perpetually white garments point to those who wash their robes in the blood of the Lamb. The "garments of salvation", as Isaiah calls them, or the "wedding garment" in the gospels – let them be white all the time: live a godly life. *"And let anointing be always on your head"* – we should always be trying to walk in the power of the Holy Spirit. When we come to church it is fairly easy to be spiritual; however, when I'm stuck on the tarmac at O'Hare Airport, about to miss a connection, my blood pressure tends to go through the ceiling! At times like those it is difficult to remember that I am still under the anointing and need to keep my garments white. When you work with an unsaved person or persons, it is very difficult to keep your garments white and oil on your head at all times. To do this we must keep the eternal perspective.

Ecclesiastes 9:9:

"Live joyfully with the wife whom you love all the days of your vain life which He has given you under the sun, all your days of vanity; for that is your portion in life, and in the labour which you perform under the sun."

Marriage was designed to be a blessing. Because of the fall of Man, however, there is a curse on the relationship between men and women that can be partially reversed in Christ. A godly marriage is a blessing – the Bible says to make the most of it. There are reasons to make the most of it: one of these reasons would be that it is one of the things that teach about eternity. Again, let's go back to the *shma: shma Israel Adonani Eloheynu adonai echad;* "Hear, O Israel, the Lord our God, the Lord is Oneness", Jesus said, quoting Moses. The oneness that takes place in marital intimacy is a picture of Christ's intimacy with His bride the Church, and God's intimacy with Israel. The kind of intimacy that takes place in a godly marriage is a small hint of the intimacy that the Church will have in eternity with Christ as a corporate Bride; this is much of what the Song of Solomon is about. But the fact that it says *"while your life is fleeting* (or vain)", well; no one stays young and good-looking forever. Romance can become a little difficult in your geriatric years, so make the most of it in your youth! God's philosophy of life is very practical. Christians can become so heavenly-minded that they're no earthly good; the Bible is never like that – rather, it deals with life for what it is. It deals with the realities of living in this world, while also dealing with what we are eternally, showing a balanced relationship between the two.

Ecclesiastes 9:10:

> "Whatever your hand finds to do, do it with your might; for there is no work or device or knowledge or wisdom in the grave where you are going."

Again, make the most of this place. You won't be here that long, so get the most eternal value out of it that you can. It's a fallen world, but make the best of your life; don't waste it. Backsliders waste their youth and they waste their lives: in comparison with eternity, what is the 80-90 years you have on this earth? Nothing. Yet in comparison with the 80-90 years you have in this world, one year, five years, ten years – these are long stretches of that time; too much time to waste on straying away from the Lord. Backsliders are the biggest time-wasters there are; everything a backslider does is a sheer waste of time and of life because none of it is of eternal value, and they know better. Continuing with verse 11:

> "I returned and saw under the sun that the race is not to the swift, nor the battle to the strong, nor bread to the wise, nor riches to Divine Aristocracy men of understanding, nor favour to men of skill; but time and chance happen to them all."

Some Christians say they don't believe in luck. However, we see here that God does. There is certainly providence – God can and does intervene on behalf of His people. Yet the fact of the matter is that due to the way of this world, the race is not always to the swift, nor is the victory always to the strong.

The only thing a cow can do is chew grass; but boy, can that cow chew it well! You will find people often who are interested in the arts, who may be multilingual, well-educated, well-travelled, and yet they struggle financially because their interests are so diverse; they have no focus. On the other hand, there are people who are not very clever, yet they open something like a gas station, work 16-hour days and save their money, and soon have two of them. How do simple people do this? Look at immigrants who come to America from countries where there is no Judeo-Christian cultural influence and no economic opportunity, only social injustice – for example, take people from India, how they'll come to England or to America and how hard they will work to get their children an education. They very often wind up with money. I stay at a Ramada Inn in the United States at times that is owned by an immigrant from India, while the janitor's great-grandparents were born there. Why is that? Because the race is not always to the swift nor the battle to the strong; time and chance overtake them all. Now, there are practical principles in the book of Proverbs for success, yet it holds true that time and chance play a significant role in this world.

One of the most brilliant founding fathers of the United States was William Morris of Pennsylvania. He foresaw how the state and the city of Philadelphia would develop, and got into land speculation. Every single thing he predicted would happen, did happen. Yet his timing on his investments was wrong, and he went bankrupt. He was a great visionary, and possibly America's first urbanologist. He saw the way things were going to develop, but his timing was all wrong. Sometimes people who are not too clever wind up with money while people who are very clever wind up broke; *"time and chance overtake them all"*. That is all the more reason not to trust in this world. If you are wealthy, maintain the attitude that you are merely God's steward, and that all your wealth is truly His to do with as He sees fit. God's philosophy is that if you are rich in material things, count yourself broke, for it belongs to Jesus rather than to you. But if you are poor, without material wealth, count yourself rich because you are a co-heir with Christ. Do not trust this world; there is no justice and no guarantee of anything, although that is not to say that God cannot and will not intervene on behalf of His people.

Continuing with Ecclesiastes 9:12:

"For man also does not know his time: like fish taken in a cruel net, like birds caught in a snare, so the sons of men are snared in an evil time, when it falls suddenly upon them."

The most successful businessperson in a city, who has worked hard and accumulated much wealth, is suddenly diagnosed with a pre-terminal disease. This sort of thing happens every day – people get caught in a snare. Unsaved people live it up, carry on as they please, but then die suddenly, and that is it for them. Now we begin to get into the aristocracy: Verses 13-18:

"This wisdom I have also seen under the sun, and it seemed great to me: There was a little city with few men in it; and a great king came against it and besieged it, and built great snares around it. Now there was found in it a poor wise man, and he by his wisdom delivered the city. Yet no one remembered that same poor man. Then I said: 'Wisdom is better than strength. Nevertheless the poor man's wisdom is despised, and his words are not heard. Words of the wise, spoken quietly, should be heard rather than the shouting of a ruler among fools. Wisdom is better than weapons of war; but one sinner destroys much good."

Let us understand this imagery of a city: We see the same imagery of a surrounded city in the fall of Samaria, in the fall of Jerusalem in 585 BC, and again in the fall of Jerusalem in 70 AD. Jerusalem, of course, is a picture of heaven in the book of Revelation. In both Hebrews and Revelation we see that earthly Jerusalem is a shadow of the heavenly Jerusalem; in fact, the writer of Hebrews calls it a copy. The city is under siege: those who knew the way out of the siege, like Elisha during the famine and siege of his time, or Jeremiah in his time, were despised. In 70 AD it was the same – after the martyrdom of James, the leader or senior pastor of the church in Jerusalem was a cousin of Jesus named Simeon. He was there when the Roman siege of Jerusalem that had been prophesied by Daniel and again by Jesus began. We can read about this in Eusebius and Josephus. God's people escaped from Jerusalem, both in Jeremiah's day and in 70 AD because they had wisdom. However, those who had wisdom were not the ones held in high esteem. Jeremiah and Simeon were looked down upon. The ones who knew how to escape were despised. In the Last Days it is the same; remember the Olivet Discourse in Matthew 24 and Luke 21 – the events of 70 AD prefigure the rapture of the church. The way the believers came out of Jerusalem and were rescued is a type of the rapture happening before the tribulation really gets bad.

Gold, silver, and jewels will not help you escape; only wisdom, knowledge and understanding will. Jesus said *"When you see Jerusalem surrounded..."* and those with wisdom knew how to interpret the signs. Eschatologically, all of this comes into play: the people who understand that wisdom is better than what the world calls strength are despised, and their wisdom is not heeded, just as the people didn't listen to Jeremiah or to the believers in 70 AD. Verse 17 again:

> "The words of the wise heard in quietness are better than the shouting of a ruler among fools."

You are better off in a home Bible study with six people where Jesus is lifted up and scripture is truly expounded than in a huge, massive church where people are rolling on the floor in hysterics, shouting, and going ape over the latest nonsense or hype. There is no wisdom in it; *"the words of the wise heard in quietness are better than the shouting of a ruler among fools"*. The word "fools" here is not *"raca"*, not a belittlement of a person's natural lack of intelligence or a mockery of someone's congenital birth defect; rather, it speaks of people who are wilfully fools, who pervert their logic. Jesus told us that if we call someone a fool due to a natural lack of intelligence we are in danger of hellfire – we are never to berate people because they are not intelligent naturally. However, when those who do know better behave foolishly, the scripture berates them in places such as Jeremiah and Ecclesiastes. When you see churches today taking part in the errors of hyper-Pentecostalism, with the shouting and hysteria and general foolishness that goes on, that is what scripture calls *"the shouting of a ruler among fools"*. You are far better off in a tiny church where there is wisdom and where the Word of God is accurately taught and explained, where someone will tell you how to escape this besieged city before it is too late.

Verse 18 tells us that *"wisdom is better than weapons of war; but one sinner destroys much good"*. I have seen this many, many times: it happens when a new church is founded, because every new work will be tested. Every time a new church is planted a lot of zeal, enthusiasm and prayer goes into it; the Lord moves and does things, but then one person comes in with his or her own agenda. That person can sink the whole ship. Sometimes it only needs one person to sow seeds of discord in a congregation and ruin it. One of the things I have learned is what the Maccabees learned: many will join us in hypocrisy in the Last Days. The fact that someone is against what you are against does not at all guarantee that they are for what you are for. Most of the people who will read Dave Hunt's books or listen to my tapes or read Bill Randles' books or things like this are sincere Christians. Many have been burned by crazy churches or exploited financially or something similar to that, yet they themselves are sincere, genuine Christians. However, there is a small percentage that will simply use good teachers or good churches as sounding boards for their own agendas. Give them enough time and they will fall out with you. These are not people who have righteous indignation and are standing against heresy or immorality; these are people who could not fit into any church. These are people with a rebellious spirit, who cannot accept any leadership or any commitment except on their own terms. Very small numbers of them can destroy a whole church. In a church of 200 people, 5 can cause a split. *"One sinner destroys much good."*

Let's continue with Ecclesiastes 10:1:

> "Dead flies make the perfumer's oil stink; so a little foolishness is weightier than wisdom and honour."

There is a foolish argument which says that because a thing is not all bad it must be good. We address this in *The Sons of Zadok*, explaining the Greek word *parasaxousin*, meaning to put truth next to error, and looking at the word *acatharsis*, meaning a mixture of truth and error, and their uses in scripture concerning a mixture of good and bad doctrine. When you hear someone saying, "We have to eat the meat and spit out the bones," you are hearing man's flawed wisdom. The Hebrews were forbidden to make a garment out of flax mixed with wool; God did not allow it. A little leaven leavens the entire lump of dough. This does not give us the right to find fault over every little doctrine, but it does require us to take a stand over the things that are fundamental.

Here in Ecclesiastes 10:1, however, this principle is described in a specific manner: *"dead flies make the perfumer's oil stink"*; fragrances in the Bible are types of worship. Remember that scripture calls the prayers of the saints incense, and that when God was angry with Israel and they offered Him burnt offerings, His response was to say "I will not smell your fragrances". So let's say I come home from Hong Kong with a bottle of duty-free perfume as a gift for my wife – only there's a fly carcass floating in it. What would have been a nice gift is ruined by one small thing. (Interestingly, the Latin philo-genetic name for a fly is *musica domestica*, or 'house music', because of the buzzing it makes.) When the carcass of a fly begins to decompose in a bottle of perfume, its enzymes interact chemically with the perfume, and this causes it to give forth a very foul odour rather than a sweet fragrance.

Again, fragrances scripturally refer to worship. I've been to church services where they are singing good choruses and good hymns, and the Holy Spirit is moving, but then they suddenly begin to go into something unbiblical – usually something pneumo-centric, directed toward the Holy Spirit, which is unbiblical since the Holy Spirit is never prayed to in the Bible. He is only prayed to or worshipped within the context of the Trinity – He Himself always points to Jesus. Our faith is Christo-centric, not pneumo-centric. In any case, back to this church service: Ten choruses or hymns are all good, and one is wrong. But it only takes one fly to spoil the ointment – the Father wants to be worshipped in Spirit and in Truth. This idea that we have to take the good with the bad is man's flawed wisdom, not God's perfect wisdom. For saying this, I am often called critical – somehow, being biblical has now become being critical. Nonetheless, this is a scriptural truth: it doesn't take more than one fly to ruin the perfume. Something that was sweet-smelling thus becomes revolting, because death is in it. Continuing with Ecclesiastes 10:2:

> "A wise man's heart directs him towards the right, but the foolish man's heart directs him towards the left."

This reminds me of what Jesus said in Matthew 25 concerning the separation of sheep and goats, sheep on His right hand and goats on His left. There are some believers who are always going towards the left; always going the wrong way. I can't explain why, but it is always the same people who follow one silly trend after another piece of nonsense and get into trouble. In England, who is taking the Alpha courses? The same people who are involved in Toronto. Who is into Pensacola? The same people who are into Promise Keepers. It's always the same people getting into weird stuff; they do it chronically.

For example: I knew a girl in England who was a lawyer. When she was in university, she would come with friends who were in the Christian fellowship on campus to some of my Bible studies in the North of England. She graduated, and eventually her friends came to one of my meetings and told me they were very concerned about her because she'd gotten involved with some group that seemed on the surface to be born-again, but were actually more like a cult. This group had persuaded her to go to Chicago with them, and her friends asked me to see what was happening to her. Several weeks later I had to be in Chicago – my wife was with me – and I found a way to contact this young woman. I had to make a deal to meet her in front of a department store because our meeting had to be surreptitious due to the extreme heavy shepherding and control this group exerted. I met her, talked with her, and took her to talk to my wife. I couldn't believe what she told me – this is an educated woman, yet this group she was in was telling people who were clean and healthy to marry people who were HIV-positive and trust the Lord to preserve their lives and health. Some of them were dying of AIDS as a result of obeying this. I took her to a mission, showed them my minister's card (this is the only reason I am ordained: so I can have a minister's license which gets me into hospitals and jails and, in my case, sometimes out of one), and got them to keep her there. I told them not to let anyone talk to her, and promised I would return the next day. Next, I called her parents (who were not saved) and told them what she was involved with. The next day, I took her to O'Hare Airport personally and put her on the plane with a stern warning that if I ever saw her there again I would do something unpleasant with my size 12 extra-wide boot. In any case, this girl went back to England. A while later she came to the Moriel church we planted in the South of England and told me she was in another crazy church. I saw her again several weeks ago, and she told me she'd been married to someone from that crazy church, but was now out of the church as well as separated from her husband.

There are just some Christians who are always like that, with one thing after another. Now, a young believer can come to Christ with a lot of baggage and get themselves into a lot of trouble – I understand that. I was saved out of the hippie movement, so I know what that's like. However, when you see people who chronically get into spiritual and doctrinal trouble, it's a serious thing. *"A wise man's heart directs him towards the right, but a foolish man's heart directs him towards the left."*

Let's continue in Ecclesiastes 10 with verses 3-5:

> "Even when a fool walks along the road his sense is lacking, and he demonstrates to everyone that he is a fool. If the ruler's temper rises against you, do not abandon your position, because composure allays great offences. There is an evil I have seen under the sun, like an error which goes forth from the ruler:"

This is a ruler from whom we should not back down; an error goes forth from him. Therefore we know that this ruler is not God or of God – no error goes forth from God, and from Him we had all better back down. This, on the contrary, is a ruler we must stand up to, from whom error comes. Obviously this is the ruler of this world, the devil; however, it is also those who operate in his character. We must link this to what was in the previous chapter (remember, there are no chapter divisions in the original text), where we are told that *"the words of the wise heard in quietness are better than the shouting of a ruler among fools"*. Ungodly leaders of the church operate in the character of Satan. Why did Jesus call the Pharisees a generation of serpents? Because Satan was also a serpent and a beguiler.

II Corinthians 11:13: *"For such men are false apostles, deceitful workers disguising themselves as apostles of Christ."* They try to look like the genuine article. *"And no wonder, for even Satan disguises himself as an angel of light; therefore it is not surprising if his servants also disguise themselves as servants of righteousness, whose end shall be according to their deeds."* Wicked leaders who come to deceive operate in the character of Satan, as Jesus describes in Matthew 23, serpents and deceivers – or as Paul states, liars trying to look like angels of light. Do not back down from such rulers any more than you would back down from Satan himself.

Notice how these rulers operate: we are told in Ecclesiastes 10:4 not to abandon our position if his temper rises. These men hate to be challenged, because they cannot respond biblically. If you are being attacked for upholding God's Word, there is a holy anger that may come on you like it did on Moses when he found the people worshipping the golden calf – but you will always be able to respond biblically. These wicked leaders cannot respond biblically, so instead they say things like "You have a rebellious spirit", "Don't you trust us?", or "You're divisive". The divisive man, according to Romans 16:17, is the one who departs from biblical truth. They get angry when you confront them, but do not back down from them.

People ask me everywhere what they should do about the state of their church or the attitude of their pastor – however, they are asking the wrong person. I am not the Holy Spirit, nor is any man, however godly; we must all ask Jesus what we should do in our particular situations. If you find yourself in a bad church, you either stay in and fight or stand up and leave. If God tells you to stay in and fight, that is what you must do; if He tells you to leave, then that is what you must do. If you stay and fight, however, expect to be thrown out. But whatever you do, do not stay in and pretend everything is all right. Don't back down from these guys who rant and rave or have people behaving like fools. *"The shouting of a ruler among fools"* – don't back down from people like that; they operate in the devil's character. False prophets are exposed and proven by their false prophecies.

Continuing with Ecclesiastes 10:5:

> "There is an evil I have seen under the sun, like an error which goes forth from the ruler: Folly is set in many exalted places, while rich men sit in humble places."

Who are the rich here? Those with knowledge, wisdom, and understanding. Who are the poor? Those who lack the same. Laodicea says "Blessed be the Lord, I have become rich and have need of nothing", not knowing that they are truly impoverished. Smyrna cries, "We're being persecuted!" – they had nothing, but Jesus told them they were rich. Again, the meek shall inherit the earth.

Think of the gospel in the same way you think of the novel by Mark Twain, *The Prince and the Pauper*. That book was based on a docu-fiction based on King Edward VI of England, son of Henry VIII. In it, Edward who was heir to the kingdom found a look-alike who by some genetic accident was the spitting image of him: a peasant boy from the streets of London. He persuaded this peasant boy to switch places with him, so the peasant began living like the prince while the prince began living like the peasant.

This teaches us a couple of things: First about Jesus – the theological term is *'kenosis'*, meaning that although He was God, Jesus came in human form, in the form of a servant. Jesus never once used His divine power while He lived here on earth, though He could have. He only did what He saw His Father doing. Satan tried to tempt Him to use His divine power, but He refused. Jesus only did what the Father did through Him by the Holy Spirit. He came in the form of a servant, identifying with us in order to save us.

Second, this novel teaches us about the present condition of the Western church: In *The Prince and the Pauper*, the prince finds himself out on the street, and although he is the genuine aristocrat, the real heir and noble, his power does him no good. The pauper begins to take the game seriously: he pretends he is really the heir to be king, and in an attempt to keep himself in that position he begins doubling the guard and other similar things. Ultimately it is straightened out, but while the pauper was playing prince, he displayed his ignorance of affairs of state. He was not groomed for a position of authority and had no understanding. For example, he did not know what the royal seal was, and was using it as a nutcracker. He did not know what he was doing, and that is exactly what we have today in the church: we have peasants in pulpits. They don't know what they are doing, though they are in the position of authority and most often are trying their best to safeguard their position. In fact, they will go so far as to prevent those who should have the position from getting it: all they are really about is self-preservation. Those who know what to do with power and resources, the true nobility, are in humble places. *"I have seen an evil under the sun"* – God calls this evil and folly: *"Folly is set in exalted places while rich men sit in humble places."* The pastor who preaches the truth has a small church, while the peasant who is churning out an endless diet of hype from his pulpit has a huge church. This is not right; God calls it evil.

Once I was watching the news in Japan, right after North Korea had fired a missile over Japan and the Americans were scrambling to stop the North Koreans. Korea was a country that could not feed its people, yet found the resources to build missiles. Countries like India and Pakistan have behaved in much the same way – they cannot feed their populations, yet they attempt to acquire weapons of mass destruction while developed countries are attempting to shut them down. To return to this news report in Japan, however, it stated that in Korea the government was distributing what it called 'New Food' to the people. This 'New Food' resembled green fettuccini, but was only 30% wheat; the other 70% of its make-up was leaves. The manufacturers put it through a chemical process in order to make it resemble pasta, but it actually had no nutritional value whatsoever. The cellulose content of this 'new food' was extremely high, and the digestive enzyme for the metabolism of cellulose is synthesised in the appendix. The human appendix, however, is too small to enable us to digest cellulose, though animals such as rabbits are able to because of their relatively large appendixes. The result was that the people who ate the 'New Food' became bloated: it gave them the sensation of fullness, of having eaten food, yet they were in reality dying of malnutrition. This is a precise parallel to what is served in many churches today: 'New Food'. What the people are fed has no nutritional value, yet because it creates a false sensation of fullness they don't know they're starving to death. All the false prophecy, verses taken out of their proper context, hype artistry, pop psychology and God knows what else is 'New Food'.

Peasants, you see, can only give out peasant food. *"Folly is set in exalted places, while rich men sit in humble places."* The people who have true wisdom and understanding tend to be found in the smaller churches, although there are exceptions. Continuing in verse 7 of Ecclesiastes 10:

"I have seen slaves riding on horses,"

The word 'slaves' here in Hebrew is *avedim*, the same word used for the Hebrews in Egypt. Slaves are figures of unsaved people – their lives are spent making bricks for Pharaoh. The New Testament tells us that a man is enslaved by that which overcomes him. Unsaved people are enslaved to their sin, but we who know the Lord and follow Him have been set free and delivered from Egypt.

"...and princes walking like slaves on the ground."

Today we see people who are enslaved to their passions and desires, riding in limousines, driving BMW's, and generally living the high life while the real aristocracy tries to get by with Fords. The aristocrat lives like a peasant, the peasant lives like a noble, and God says that this is an evil under the sun. Verse 8:

> "He who digs a pit may fall into it, and a serpent may bite him who breaks through a wall. He who quarries stones may be hurt by them, and he who splits logs may be endangered by them. If the axe is dull and he does not sharpen its edge, he must exert more strength. Wisdom has the advantage of giving success."

In I Peter 2:5 we see that the house we build is the church, and we are the living stones of the Temple. We explain in our *Typology of the Temple* teaching how this works: we are the stones of the Temple; its components are figures of different Christians. When you chopped logs in the ancient world you used an axe; but if the blade was dull, it took more energy and force to chop the logs – it would not cut smoothly or easily, and you would also have projectiles flying in your face as it splintered. Remember the Old Testament story of how the axe-head floated: he had the axe handle, but because it had no blade, or in other words because there was no wisdom, it was ineffective and even unusable. Notice how many churches today go from one program to the next, trying to build something. Yet what is built is shabby: the stones are not evenly cut, and nothing fits together properly. You are better off in a church of 100 people that is solid and well built than in one of these huge things that fall to bits at a breath of wind. For example, what happened to the church in Pensacola, Florida, that was headquarters of the famous so-called revival? It split. What's left of Toronto, where a similar false revival was held? Practically nothing. The one in England was Sunderland; it is now a small group meeting in a hotel. They crumble, because the stones were never fitted together. There was much energy, exertion and hype put into these movements, but they came to nothing. Why? Because the head of the axe is dull – there is no wisdom.

Continuing in verse 11:

> "If the serpent bites before being charmed, there is no profit for the charmer."

Remember, *the serpent beguiled the woman;* Satan is a deceiver. I have a photo of myself in India attempting to charm a serpent. I played the flute, opening with a rendition of *Blue Suede Shoes*. The snake seemed to take exception to this and became cantankerous, so I switched to

Amazing Grace in order to calm it down. A serpent can kill you; spiritual seduction is deadly. Where is discernment? If you don't know how to charm the serpent, it will bite you. In America, they really only have one very dangerous rattlesnake in the Southwest, and then they have a cotton-mouth. These are tame garden snakes in comparison with some I have seen in Australia and Africa, or in Israel. America really doesn't have bad snakes.

These churches with an emphasis on experientialism talk very much about the gifts of the Spirit; so where is their gift of discernment? Why are they unable to charm the serpent? They are fooling around with a powerful enemy, which has the potential to kill with its bite; snakes are known to burrow into houses, into the walls unnoticed. Spiritual seduction operates in the same manner. *"If the serpent bites before being charmed, there is no profit for the charmer."* It's too late to charm a snake after it has done the damage it is capable of; the flock must be protected ahead of time.

Ecclesiastes 10:12:

> "Words from the mouth of a wise man are gracious, while the lips of a fool consume him. The beginning of his talking is folly, and the end of it is wicked madness."

Compare this with what we read in chapter 9:3: *"The hearts of the sons of men are filled with evil and insanity."* The end of his speech is "wicked madness"; more than simply madness, it is wicked madness. For a good example of this, watch our video of Rodney Howard-Browne and Kenneth Copeland. When Mr Howard-Browne begins talking, his words are foolishness; he talks nonsense. Yet the end of it is exactly what the scripture describes: wicked madness. The fruit of the Spirit is self-control, not the wicked madness that these people were led into by those men. It was actually demonic. You have to be out of your mind to do the things these people will do – the only unsaved people I have ever seen who will participate in the kinds of things so-called Christian people were doing in Pensacola, Toronto, and the imitators of such places, were Hindus practising Kundalini yoga – Kundalini meaning "serpent spirit" – and headhunters in Indonesia. In England we have many believers from India, former Hindus and Sikhs who came to Jesus. When we showed the videos of Toronto and Pensacola behaviour to the Indian pastors who'd come out of

Hinduism, they immediately identified it as Kundalini yoga, a practice they had been delivered out of by Jesus. *"Wicked madness"*. When they speak, it begins foolishly, with no doctrine given or exposition of God's Word; it inevitably ends in wicked madness.

Verse 14 of chapter 10:

> "Yet the fool multiplies words. No man knows what will happen; who can tell what will come after him? The toil of a fool so wearies him that he does not even know how to go to the city!"

Do we realise what this means? What is the city? Jerusalem, or heaven, drawing from Revelation 21. These people reach the point where they don't even know how to be saved. Jack Deere of the Vineyard movement could not explain the gospel. In England, a poll was performed of 200 people who had taken Alpha courses; of these 200, four could explain the gospel in New Testament terms – justification by faith, salvation by grace, etc. – four out of 200 knew what the gospel was. They don't even know the way to the city. Today's Charismatic movement is composed largely of people who were never even saved, particularly since Wimber taught his "cheap grace" doctrine, because the gospel is not even explained to people any more. They don't know the way to the city, and this is very frightening. Verse 16:

> "Woe to you, O land, whose king is a lad and whose princes feast in the morning. But blessed are you, O land, whose king is of nobility and whose princes eat at the appropriate time, for strength and not for drunkenness."

We are now talking about the aristocracy, the nobility. *"Blessed are you, O land, whose king is of nobility"* – what is nobility? Wisdom, knowledge, and understanding. *"But cursed is the land whose prince is a youth , 'whose king is a lad and whose princes feast in the morning'"*. To realise what this means we must keep in mind Paul's warning not to appoint a new convert as a leader in the church. Whenever I hear of someone who has been saved for one or two years and is already attending or thinking of attending seminary, my first question is 'What for?' Those who profit from theological seminary training are those who have already been operating in ministry and know their gifts. A scholarly education in academic theology is an asset to someone who already has that ministry and that gift, but it will not impart that ministry or that gift to one who has not been given it by God.

Now, God does not count youth biologically; rather, He counts youth spiritually. You may have someone who grew up in a believing family, who perhaps became saved at the age of six or so, and by the time he's 25 that man is no longer a youth. He may be spiritually and emotionally quite capable of coming into leadership. On the other hand, you may have someone who is 60 years old and newly saved who in God's sight is a youth. The scripture therefore is not speaking of biological youth, but of spiritual youth. *"Woe to you whose king is a lad"*. When you see young believers put into positions of leadership, look out, because you will certainly have a problem. Paul says they will be swollen with conceit.

And yet, *"blessed are you, O land, whose king is of the nobility and whose princes eat at the appropriate time, for strength and not drunkenness"*. This refers exactly to Matthew 24, the Olivet Discourse. Let's look at that, beginning in verse 45: *"Who, then, is the faithful and sensible servant whom his master put in charge of his household, to give them the proper food at the proper time. Blessed is that slave, whom his master finds so doing when he comes. Truly I say to you, he will put him in charge of all his possessions"* – this alludes to the millennium – *"but if that evil servant says in his heart, 'My master is not coming', and shall begin to beat his fellow slaves and eat and drink with drunkards,"* – beating the fellow slaves is Nicolaitanism, or heavy shepherding as seen in Ezekiel 44.

Jesus hated this. Heavy shepherding is done by control freaks, and of course goes hand-in-hand with financial exploitation and many other evils. But let us look at what happens: as we saw in Ecclesiastes, when the king and the princes are of the nobility they eat for strength and not for drunkenness. Being "drunk in the Spirit" is a very popular thing with those who are into the Toronto and Pensacola types of movements. If we look at Joel chapter 1, we read *"awake, ye drunkards"*; three times in Peter's first epistle, he says *"be sober in spirit"*, not drunk. In this light, we may understand better how demonic the doctrines and practices of Rodney Howard-Browne, Kenneth Copeland, and the others like them truly are. Drunkenness is one of the specific seductions of the Last Days. They are peasant rulers; God's rulers are of the nobility.

These peasant rulers may have all the gold, silver and jewels now, but that will certainly be corrected in the millennium, and they will never possess the real treasures of wisdom, knowledge and understanding. They will never know how to get people out of the city when it is under siege, or charm the serpent before it bites. They are peasants, and how can a peasant know how to run an economy? In England and in the USA there are lotteries; a study was done and published in a serious newspaper, which showed that most of the people who gamble are working-class, or blue-collar people, who are usually less educated. There is nothing wrong with being blue-collar or less educated, but it is a fact that most of the people who gamble are. When these people won the lottery, most of them were broke within ten years. They were swimming in money, but lacked the education to manage and invest it properly. Giving a peasant money is wrong and unwise; first they should be taught to manage it.

Continuing in Ecclesiastes 10:18:

> "Because of laziness the building decays, and through idleness of hands the house leaks."

Remember that Laodicea is lukewarm; it is lax and lazy, so it eventually caves in. Verse 19:

> "Men prepare a meal for enjoyment, and wine makes life merry; but money is an answer to everything."

Practically, money does solve problems; however, the wrong people usually seem to have it. We must remember verse 7, *"peasants ride on horses while princes walk like slaves"*; God has provided all of the money and resource that the Body of Christ needs for God's work, but it has been misallocated. The peasants have pilfered the treasury. One of the reasons we have TBN, Hinn and Copeland is that it is Satan's way of taking the money that should be going into missions and evangelism and squandering it on nonsense. Verse 20:

> "Furthermore, in your bedchamber do not curse the king" – remember, we are all kings, with Christ as the King of kings – "and in your sleeping-room do not curse a rich man, for a bird of the heavens will carry the sound and a winged creature will make the matter known."

Ultimately this points to God, of course, and yes, we must be careful what we think or say about God. However, this also means that when peasants say things about you, you will know about it. They are just peasants: people who do not have wisdom, understanding, or knowledge of God's Word. They are not the nobility. Again, as Jesus said to the Laodicean church: *"You say you are rich and have need of nothing, not knowing that you are wretched, pitiable, poor, blind and naked."* Yet the church of Smyrna, persecuted and materially poor, Jesus called rich; they were the nobility. Gold, silver and jewels will not get you out of the besieged city, nor will they get you into the eternal city. The church of today, Laodicea, does not know the way to that heavenly city.

God calls it an evil that princes walk while slaves ride in BMWs. Wisdom is better than material wealth; and *"the words of the wise heard in quietness are better than the shouting of a ruler among fools"*. You are always better off in a small church that teaches the truth than in a large one that feeds on hype. The serpent will bite these peasant rulers; their structure will spiritually cave in. Yet God has a nobility: He does not call His people to be peasants; He has an aristocracy. As in the story of *The Prince and the Pauper*, we may not be in practical possession of the treasures yet, but they belong ultimately to the faithful: the meek shall inherit the earth. The way it is now is an evil; but it is an evil that will be corrected by God.

Those who are in control for now are peasants, without wisdom, understanding, or knowledge; but God does have a nobility. Sometimes for now the princes walk instead of ride; sometimes the nobility is in the small church rather than the big one. You are more likely to find the rich man sitting in a humble place, while the peasant sits in the exalted place. You are more likely to find the rich man walking while the peasant rides in a limo; but the noble is still a noble and the peasant is still a peasant. The peasant knows he is a peasant, though he may successfully delude himself with his false riches for a time. A peasant can be nothing other than a peasant, and a noble can be nothing other than a noble. When the city is under siege, then we will discover who is rich and who is poor. When persecution and opposition come, the nobility and peasantry are revealed for whom they really are. When the serpent bites, it is clear who's who.

"Woe to you, O land, whose king is a lad and whose princes feast in the morning; but blessed are you, O land, whose king is of the nobility and whose princes eat at the appropriate time, for strength and not for drunkenness."

The Lord does not call you to be a peasant. Our ruler is a noble king, and He has given you blue blood. He has called you to be in His aristocracy. He wants you to claim your treasure. It is waiting for you – you are entitled to it because He has bequeathed it. He has told us what to do: go after the wealth – don't be a peasant. Gain control of the wealth that is yours, and let the peasants have what perishes. To you the Lord would say, "Take My instruction, and not silver. Take knowledge of Me and of My Word rather than choice gold. For wisdom is better than jewels, and all desirable things cannot compare with her".

You are of the nobility. You are of the aristocracy, though it may not be evident yet. The time is coming, however, when all will see who is rich and who is poor.

The Grain Offering

"When anyone presents a grain offering as an offering to the Lord, his offering shall be of fine flour. He shall pour oil on it and shall put frankincense upon it. He shall then bring it to Aaron's sons the priests, and shall take from it his handful of its fine flour, and its oil with all of its frankincense. And the priests shall offer it up in smoke as its memorial portion on the altar, an offering by fire of a soothing aroma to the Lord. "And the remainder of the grain offering belongs to Aaron and his sons, a thing most holy of the offerings to the Lord by fire. When you bring an offering of the grain offering baked in an oven, it shall be unleavened cakes of fine flour mixed with oil, or unleavened wafers spread with oil. And if your offering is a grain offering made on the griddle, it shall be of fine flour, unleavened, mixed with oil. You shall break it into bits and pour oil on it; it is a grain offering. Now, if your offering is a grain offering made in a skillet, it shall be made with fine flour and with oil. And when you bring in the grain offering, which is made of these things to the Lord, it shall be presented to the Lord by way of the priest, and he shall bring it to the altar. The priest shall then take it up from the grain offering its memorial portion, and shall offer it up in smoke on the altar as an offering by fire of a soothing aroma to the Lord. And the remainder of the grain offering belongs to Aaron and his sons, a thing most holy of the offerings to the Lord by fire. "No grain offering which you bring to the Lord shall be made with leaven, for you shall not offer up in smoke any leaven or any honey as an offering by fire to the Lord. As an offering of firstfruits you shall bring them to the Lord, but they shall not ascend for a soothing aroma on the altar. "Every grain offering of yours, moreover, you shall season with salt, so that the salt of the covenant of your God shall not be lacking from your grain offering. With all of your offerings, you shall offer salt. Also, if you bring a grain offering of early-ripened things to the Lord, you shall bring fresh heads of roasted grain in the fire, grits of new

MORE GRAIN FOR THE FAMINE

growth, for the grain offering of your early-ripened things. You shall
then put oil on it, and lay incense on it; it is a grain offering. And the
priest shall offer up in smoke its memorial portion, a portion of its grits,
of its oil, and all of its incense as an offering by fire to the Lord"
(Leviticus 2:1).

eviticus in Hebrews is *V'yekra*, or 'And Yahweh Called'. Most
Christians have some kind of an idea that the animal sacrifices
of the Old Testament — what Jewish people call the *Tenakh* —
are symbols of Jesus. They might know that the Passover lamb, the
lamb without blemish, is a picture of what Jesus would be; that to
God, one man without sin is worth more than all the men with sin,
and that is how one Man could die for us all. Some people might also
know about the Yom Kippur scapegoat on the Day of Atonement; we
read about this in the epistle to the Hebrews chapters 9 - 11. The high
priest would actually put his hands on two goats, and put the sin in
symbol upon their heads. They would then take the goats through the
streets, where the people would spit on them, kick them, throw rocks
at them, beat them with sticks and curse them for their sin. The goats
would then be escorted outside the city, where one would be
slaughtered and the other taken to a precipice. It was a symbol of what
would happen to Jesus: God would put our sin on Him; He would be
paraded through the streets of Jerusalem, taken outside the city and
executed. Most Christians have an idea that the blood sacrifices of
these animals were symbols of Jesus; however, most Christians do not
think about the grain offering.

Paul, whose real name was Rabbi Shaul of Tarsus, tells us that we
establish the Torah — the five books of Moses, which are fulfilled in
Jesus. All of these things point to Him. You can understand the gospel
and know how to be saved just in reading the New Testament. But to
understand it on a deeper level, to understand the fullness of the
gospel, you must understand it in light of its Old Testament
background. We have to understand how Jesus fulfilled the Law.

The grain offering here is what we call in Hebrew *'matzoth'* —
unleavened. Perhaps you have seen matzoth; some churches use
matzoth for communion. It is striped and it is pierced; the Talmud
decrees that the unleavened bread used at Passover has to be so. This

94

corresponds, the rabbis tell us, with the flesh of the Passover lamb. This is exactly what Jesus speaks about in John chapter 6; it is a picture of His body. So the bread was striped, and then pierced, and then broken. *"By His stripes we are healed"*, and *"He was pierced for our transgressions"*, the Hebrew prophet Isaiah tells us. The grain offering is a symbol of the sacrifice of Jesus for our sins.

The grain could be offered in three ways: First, it would be offered on an open fire, on a griddle. Second, it would be offered in a skillet — a kind of pan with a long handle. The third way would be what we call in Hebrew *b'tanur*; inside an oven. The grain would be offered on an open fire, in a skillet, and in an oven. We are three-dimensional beings, because we are made in the image and likeness of God; *Imago Dei*. We have a body, a soul, and a spirit. That is one of the things about our nature that teaches how we are made in the image and likeness of a tri-une God. The threeness in us expresses something about the threeness in our Creator. We are what people would call 'theopomorphic'; in the image and likeness of God.

Given that fact, we can see that when Jesus died for our sin, He had to suffer in body, in soul, and in spirit. Sin contaminates every aspect of our being: it contaminates our flesh, or our body; it contaminates our soul, or our mind, emotions, and intellect; and it contaminates our spirit. Every aspect of our being is fallen because of sin. Therefore, in order to take away our sin, Jesus had to atone for it in body, in soul, and in spirit.

So: the first sacrifice of the grain is that which is offered on the open fire. When the grain was offered on the griddle, everyone could see it being consumed. This corresponds to the physical suffering of the Lord Jesus. There He was, enduring a Roman execution, hanging nearly naked in public; everyone could see Him being tortured physically. When they nailed Him to the cross, He was nailed there for my sin. When the Romans flogged Him and put the crown of thorns on His head, it was because He took my sin. Jesus got the nails; I got salvation. The just for the unjust.

There is a big problem in the American Bible belt, and here is what that problem is: cultural Protestantism. In other words, you have people who will go to churches that preach the gospel and believe the gospel only because they have grown up in it; they've always done it. Yet they have never come to be saved. This is a big problem, which I have seen all over the world where there are Bible belts: I've seen it in South Africa, in Northern Ireland, and certainly in the American south. The doctrines are there; the beliefs are there; but some of the people may know the Lord, while others may not. When Jesus went to that cross, He went for you. God took your sin and put it on Jesus; He took His righteousness and put it on you. You must accept this personally, or you are not a Christian, no matter how many times you come to church.

He suffered in body; everyone could see the grain being burned up. His torture was unspeakable. I once read an autopsy report done by some Christian pathologists who did post-mortems on cadavers which had been crucified in the Roman style, and it was incredibly horrible. Even with modern technology, we would be hard put to find a more cruel way to kill somebody than the way in which the Romans killed Jesus.

The grain was also offered up, however, in a skillet. When the grain was consumed in the skillet, what was happening was only partially visible. You could see some of what was going on, but you could not see all of it. This grain being burned up in the skillet, as per Leviticus chapter 2, corresponds to the emotional/psychological suffering of Jesus; what the Bible calls 'the travail of His soul'.

When someone is suffering emotionally or psychologically — if someone is perhaps in depression, or bereaved, or being oppressed in some way — other people can see some of what is going on with that person, but not all of it. You could only see some of the grain being consumed in the skillet at a distance. In order to see the totality of its being burned up, you would have had to stand directly above it and look down. So it is when someone is suffering emotionally, whether they are in a depression or bereaved or perhaps grieving the lostness of an unsaved loved one, other people can see some of what that person is going through, but only He who looks down from above can see all of it. The Lord knows everything; other people can only appreciate some of it, and perhaps empathise; but God sees it all.

You see, Jesus took our griefs; He suffered psychologically. He was emotionally and mentally tortured.

But then there was a third way in which the grain was consumed: this is again in Hebrew, *b'tanur*, or 'inside the oven'. This was not visible to anybody.

When Jesus went to the cross, something happened within the tri-unity of the Godhead itself: the Father turned His back on the Son. Now, we must be careful; there is a terrible heresy that originated in the American south, which is propagated by the money preachers on so- called "Christian" television. They call it "Jesus died spiritually". It is an absolute blasphemous lie, which says that Satan got the victory at the cross, and that when Jesus died, although He Himself said, "It is finished", and "Father, into Your hands I commend My spirit", it didn't happen. That instead, He became a satanic being of one nature with Satan in hell, where He was then tortured for three days and three nights, until He was born again — still in hell. This is what the money preachers believe. So, because the cross of Jesus is not central to their view of the Christian life, neither do they view the cross of Jesus as central to salvation. Instead of "Pick up your cross and follow Me, and put your trust in a better world," their beliefs consist of "Name-it-and-claim-it, you're a King's kid, God wants you rich", and Kingdom Now, etc. This is a terrible heresy; Jesus got the victory on the cross, not the devil. However, something did happen in that oven. Something did happen within the Godhead. The Father turned His back on the Son; God could not look upon sin. We do not fully understand what happened.

We cannot for one second diminish the physical suffering of Jesus; His agony was excruciating. Neither can we diminish His emotional and mental suffering; scripture speaks plainly of the 'travail of His soul', that is also true. But the deeper suffering of Jesus was what happened within the Trinity; the Father turning His back on the Son. Something happened in that oven. How can God have a crisis in Himself, where the Father turns His back on the Son because the Son took our sin in order to give us His righteousness? Terrible as His physical suffering was, excruciating as his emotional torment was, what happened spiritually was even worse. Jesus was cut off at that moment from His Father, for my sin and for your sin.

He suffered in body, in soul, and in spirit. Thus the grain had to be offered: in the griddle, where everyone could see it; in the skillet, where it could partially be seen and only fully observed from above; and in the oven, where no one could see it.

Now, this grain had to be anointed. It had to have oil poured upon it. The basic Hebrew word for 'oil' is *shemen*; it speaks of anointing.

The word 'Christ' comes from the Greek word *christos*, and is the Greek way of saying the Hebrew term *ha Mashiach*, or 'the Anointed One', or the Messiah. Jesus was anointed for burial before He was anointed for dominion. When Paul speaks of the proof for his anointing and his ministry in 2 Corinthians, he does not speak first of the miracles or of the signs of an apostle. He first speaks of having been abandoned, shipwrecked, stoned, etc, etc. The first and foremost proof of a real anointing, an anointing that comes from Christ, is a crucified life. It is a life lived without trust in this world. It is certainly not a Mercedes limousine, nor the kind of material extravagance which we see on the so-called "Christian" television, which the world looks at and mocks. That is not anointing; anointing is a crucified life, lived by someone who does not trust in this life or this world, but who will trust God for the grace to suffer anything that they need to if it is in God's will; someone who does not love their life in this world, even if it should come to death. That is the true proof of anointing.

Jesus was anointed for burial; the oil was poured on the grain. Oil and frankincense; when Jesus was born, the Magi brought gold because He was a King, myrrh because He would die (myrrh, you remember, is what dead bodies were anointed with for burial, as we read in John 19:39), and also frankincense because incense, we are told in Revelation, is the prayers of the saints.

To understand what this means, let us look very briefly at the Song of Solomon chapter four verse six. We call the Song of Solomon in Hebrew *Hashir Hashirim*, and it is an allegory. Solomon's romance with Shulammite is a picture of Christ's romance with His bride. We are told this in chapter four verse six:

"Until the cool of the day comes,
When the shadows flee away,
I will go my way to the mountain of myrrh,
To the hill of frankincense."

The bridegroom is anointed for burial to die for the bride, to bring the acceptable sacrifice on the mountain of myrrh, the mountain that we would call Mount Calvary. So He is anointed for burial in order to bring the acceptable sacrifice. You see, you can pray and pray and pray, sing hymn after hymn after hymn, and it does not matter. Unless it is in Christ, unless you are born again, God cannot accept your worship. It is only what is done in Christ that matters. You can go to church all you want, and that is good; but it is not good enough. Only in Christ does it matter. But let us continue.

So the grain was anointed to bring the acceptable worship. It had oil and it had incense; but the grain could have no honey. It could also have no leaven; this is what *'matzoth'* means: "unleavened bread". Why could this bread, which is a picture of the body of Jesus, have no leaven? What is leaven? The New Testament tells us repeatedly what leaven is.

In 1 Corinthians 5, Paul tells us the following: *"Your boasting is not good. Do you not know that a little leaven leavens the entire lump of dough? Leave behind the old leaven that you might be a new lump, just as you are in fact unleavened. For the Messiah our Pesach, Christ our Passover, has been sacrificed."*

Leaven, or yeast, contributes nothing whatsoever to the nutritional value of bread. It only puffs it up; *"your boasting is not good"*. The first thing that leaven speaks of is sin, but especially the sin of pride. Pride is the seminal sin; it is the sin that gives rise to other sin. In Isaiah chapter 14 we are told that the first sin was pride. Satan wanted to be God; in eternity, Satan wanted to usurp God's position. Pride was Satan's first sin, according to Isaiah 14. During the temptation of Adam and Eve, man's first sin was pride. Pride is the kind of sin that leads to other sin. When you see someone who has a problem with greed, pride is underneath that greed. When you see a person who has a problem with uncontrolled lust, underneath that lust is pride. When you see a person who has a problem with unrighteous, unholy anger, underneath that anger is pride. Pride is the seminal sin; it gives rise to other sin.

The only thing I have to be proud of is what Jesus did for me on the cross; that is all. That He took my sin and rose from the dead is the only thing I have to be proud of. Jesus, however, was God, and He had no sin. He had everything to be proud of; yet He who had something to be proud of was not proud. I who have nothing to be proud of have to battle with pride every day; so do you. We battle it every day, but Jesus had none. There was no leaven in that *matzoth*.

But then he spoke further: *"Beware of the leaven of the Pharisees."* False doctrine. When you see heresy and false doctrine (and all you have to do to see false doctrine is to turn on the so-called "Christian" television; it consists of much more false doctrine than true doctrine), this is the leaven of the Pharisees. It puffs up; there is pride. "God showed me, I can do this, we're going to go forth and conquer" — spiritual pride. Whenever you see false doctrine and heresy, the source of it is always spiritual pride. Beware of the leaven of the Pharisees. Jesus had no false doctrine, no heresy. Every word that He taught was one hundred and ten per cent true. There was no leaven in that *matzoth*. If there had been, he would not have been able to die for our sins.

Once more: to God, one man without sin is worth more than all men with sin. It doesn't matter how good you are; you're not good enough to go to heaven. On the other hand, it does not matter how bad you are; you're not so bad that God does not love you and Jesus cannot take your sin and give you His life. That is the gospel.

It is difficult when people have grown up hearing it their whole lives; they go to good churches for 20, 30, 40 years and hear this message — or variations of it — some of them probably hundreds of times. Yet they have still never been born again; that is a terrible tragedy. My family are Israeli Jews; Jews are more guilty than other people for rejecting the gospel, because Jesus was Jewish and because the gospel came to Israel first. It says in Romans that God holds the Jews accountable first. Because salvation is available to them first, the consequences of rejecting it are on them first, we're told in Romans. So, too, people who have heard the gospel repeatedly are going to be more accountable than people who do not live in places where it is as readily available. I never knew what a born-again Christian was until I was in university; I had never even heard of such a thing. But many people have grown up hearing about it without accepting it. They know the truth; or at least they have the truth available to them. I go to Africa, India, the Middle East; I go to places where the people have never heard the truth. Yet there are people who go to church and hear it Sunday after Sunday after Sunday, but their lives don't change.

There was no leaven — no pride, no false doctrine — in that matzoh. One man with no sin could die for all the men with sin.

But then there could be no honey. Why could there be no honey on that grain? What is the problem with honey? We know what leaven is — the scriptures tell us. But what is wrong with honey? Why does God say in Leviticus chapter 2 that there could be no honey on the grain when it was sacrificed?

Look, please, to the book of Proverbs chapter 24:13. We must always interpret scripture in light of other scripture. This is what we read: *"My son, eat honey, for it is good. Yes, the honey from the comb is sweet to your taste."* Honey is sweet. Let us understand the Hebrew thought in the idea of honey: Honey in Hebrew is called *devash*, because it comes from the Hebrew word for 'bee', *devorah*. The girl's name 'Deborah' means 'bee' in Hebrew. But the Hebrew word for the Bible, the Word of God, is *devar*. The Word of God is sweet. Remember in the book of Revelation, or in Ezekiel chapter 3, that the scroll was sweet in the mouth yet bitter in the stomach. The Word of God is sweet to us; it tastes sweet. Yet the Word of God should always be sweet in our mouths, yet bitter in our gut. It can be very interesting and very encouraging; but we are also responsible for it. It is not given simply to increase our knowledge, but to change our lives. It is sweet in the mouth, but bitter in the gut. You see, we only like the honey bits. We don't like the bitter bits.

The Hebrews entered a land of milk and honey, and one day, so shall we. Heaven will be a land of milk and honey; the Promised Land. One is a picture of the other. In heaven, everything will be lovey-dovey. However, in the meantime we have come out of Egypt — a picture of the world — and we are sojourning in the wilderness. The desert is a difficult place. The manna fell for Israel, and it tasted like honey; now, the manna falls and it tastes like honey.

But there is a problem with honey. Not with the honey in itself, but in what we do with it. Look at Proverbs 25:16: *"Have you found honey? Eat only what you need, lest you have it in excess and vomit it."* Too much honey makes us sick. I myself am very moderately Pentecostal/Charismatic, though I am against all of the extremism. But I will tell you one of the things that has gone wrong with the Pentecostal movement, and why after almost 30 years it has brought no revival: too much honey. Everything was based on affection and feeling and being lovey-dovey. They wanted only the sweet in the mouth, not the bitter in the gut. They embraced experiential theology instead of biblical theology. Their doctrine comes from what they make up as they go along because it feels good to them; it is the same as secular psychology. The feel-good factor: 'if it feels good, it must be right'.

"Eat what you need" — you need a certain amount of honey. We all need affection; honey speaks of affection. The two kinds of parents who will most seriously damage their children spiritually and emotionally are the ones who are overly strict and the ones who are overly permissive. I had an uncle who was in the American military, and his position was in training soldiers for combat. He was a hero in Korea, and a good soldier; but he could not separate his professional life from his family life. As a result, he was overly strict with his children, and regimented them. This damaged them, and one after another they went wrong. Ultimately they were responsible for their own lives, but their upbringing was overly strict. Do you know that there are fathers who have never hugged their children? The Bible speaks more of a father's love than it does of a mother's love, because God is a father figure. If a child has never seen the love of a father, that lack is going to obscure his or her view of God. There are fathers who never show much-needed affection to their children.

Yet 'eat only what you need'; don't consume too much. "Oh, don't smack little Henry; Henry is a good boy"; until one day, the police knock on the door when little Henry is no longer so little — nor so good.

Have you found honey? Eat what you need; we do need honey. But too much will make us sick. Be careful of people who are ruled by their emotions, who substitute emotion and feeling for spirituality. It is the teaching of the Word of God that determines what is spiritual; our feelings do not.

Let us look further: Proverbs 25:27: *"It is not good to eat much honey; nor is it glory to search out one's own glory."* When you see people eating too much honey — who are ruled by their emotions — these are people who are into spiritual pride. They are seeking their own glory, believing they are more spiritual than others around them, embracing the attitude of 'holier-than-thou', and for them, feeling and emotion wrongly become the barometer of spirituality. "Oh, we don't judge! We don't criticise!"

My own family is a combination of two backgrounds: Jewish and Catholic. We have Jewish families who are on their way to hell without their Messiah, yet there are Christians who claim to love the Jews while refusing to give them the gospel. There are actual organisations, which call themselves 'Christian Embassies', composed of people who want to bring the Jews back to Israel; yet they will withhold the gospel from them in the name of 'love'. What they are actually saying is, "We love you, Jew! Go to hell." No; if you love Jews, tell them about the Messiah.

"Oh, we love our Catholic brethren!" I have a mother who trusts in a statue of Mary for her salvation instead of in the Lord Jesus Christ; my mother is on her way to hell. If we love Catholics, we will tell them the true gospel. Either the blood of Christ cleanses you from all sin, or you are going to atone in purgatory for your own; which gospel are you going to believe? Paul said that if an angel of God came preaching another gospel, we are to reject him. There is no purgatory; we do not atone for our own sin, because the blood of Christ cleanses from all sin. Yet in the name of love, people will claim Catholics as brethren and leave them in bondage to the fear of death. This is not love; perfect love casts out all fear. Jesus took our sin; yet in the name of love, certain Christians will leave people in that bondage. "Oh, but we have to love the Catholics!" Certainly we do; so let us tell them the truth! In Philippians 1:9 we see that love and truth are not mutually exclusive, but rather are mutually dependent. Yet because the Charismatic movement runs on honey instead of on grain, they no longer know this.

"Eat what you need; not too much."

The functions of the soul are the mind, the intellect, and the emotions. Human intellect is a very good servant, but it is a bad master. Human emotion is also a very good servant, but it is a deadly, cruel, lethal master. When you find people who are thinking with their emotions, and substituting feeling for the Word of God, you are looking at people who are into spiritual pride and are on a suicide trip spiritually. They will also take others down with them if allowed to do so.

No, there was no honey on that grain. There was no emotion involved in the crucifixion of Jesus. The Father turned His back on His Son. No; *I* got the honey — 'God so loved the world . . .' — I got the honey. The girls I slept with, the cocaine I scooped up my nose — Jesus paid the price for that. He got the nails; He was nailed to a tree for what I did, and I got the honey. He did not get any honey; there was no honey on that grain.

There could be no honey, and no leaven. Leviticus 2:12: *"An offering of the firstfruits you shall bring to the Lord, but they shall not ascend for a soothing aroma on the altar."* Why could the grain of the firstfruit not be used as a grain offering? Understand what the firstfruit meant: it was a Hebrew feast during Passover week, in April. Jesus was crucified at that time; but on the Sunday of that week, the high priest would go into the Kidron Valley, which lies directly between the Temple Mount and the Mount of Olives. Exactly at sunrise, when he saw the first ray of light coming up from in back of the Mount of Olives illuminating the first shoot of grain, that would be called the firstfruit. The high priest would then ceremonially harvest it and bring it into the temple; that would be the firstfruit. All four gospels tell us that Jesus rose around dawn; in other words, at the very hour at which the high priest was bringing the firstfruit into the temple, Jesus was rising from the dead as the firstfruit of the resurrection. This is what Paul tells us in I Corinthians 15:20: *"But now Christ has been raised from the dead, the firstfruits of those who are asleep."* He is the Firstfruit.

So the grain of the firstfruit could not be put on the altar and sacrificed. Why? Because Jesus died once and for all. Once He had died for our sin and risen from the grave, He would never die again. This is why, when Moses struck the rock more than once, he could not enter the Promised Land. It was like crucifying Jesus repeatedly. He died once, and then the Living Water — the Holy Spirit — came.

There is a big problem today called ecumenism. Now, for saved Christians to unite with saved Christians is very good. I am all for born- again Baptists getting together with born-again Presbyterians and born- again Pentecostals (if they are not extreme). I am in favour of saved Christians uniting. But when saved Christians begin getting into bed with liberal Protestants, unbelievers; when saved Christians begin getting into bed with the Roman Catholic church; that is something quite different. Let's look at what it says in Hebrews 7:27: *"We do not need daily a high priest like those high priests, to offer up sacrifices for his own sin and then for the sins of the people, because this Jesus did once and for all"* He died one time. In Hebrews 9:12 we read the same thing: *"And not through the blood of goats and calves, but through His own blood He entered the holy place once and for all."* And in Hebrews 9:28: *"So that Christ also, having been offered once to bear the sins of many".* Hebrews 10:10: *"By this we will have been sanctified: the offering of the body of Jesus Christ once and for all."* Verse 14 of chapter 10: *"For by one offering He has perfected for all time those who are sanctified."* One time; if something has been perfected, it cannot be improved upon. Jesus died once and only once.

Therefore, He is the Firstfruit, we are told in Corinthians. He died once, rose from the dead once, never to die again, because His sacrifice was perfect. The Roman Catholic doctrine of the mass denies this, claiming that the mass is the same sacrifice as Calvary, and that Jesus dies again and again and again. The Catholic doctrine of the mass is a fundamental denial of the gospel of Jesus Christ.

The Reformers were certainly not perfect men. Luther, Calvin, Zwingli — they made a lot of mistakes, and they even persecuted Baptists. However, every one of them was a Roman Catholic priest who got saved when he read the Bible. Not only were they from the Roman Catholic clergy, but they were from the intelligentsia of the Roman Catholic clergy. When they went back and read the scriptures in the original Greek languages, they understood what was wrong. Every one of the Reformers was a Roman Catholic priest who read the scriptures in the original language and got saved. Those doctrines have not changed: Jesus died once and for all.

The grain had to be salted. Again we come back to this idea of the Word. John chapter 1, *"In the beginning was the Word"*. Jesus is the Word, and the Bible is the Word. His Word is Him; it is salty. Salt was the only preservative they had in the ancient Near East. The Word of God — the salt — preserves. The power of Jesus preserves. If a church stops being evangelistic, it will eventually stop being evangelical. If you abandon Christ, you will eventually abandon His Word; and that is where liberal Protestantism has gone. They 'hold a form of religion, but deny the power therein'. They want to keep only the moral teachings of the Bible, forgetting the personal relationship with the Lord. The Word is the Word; once the Word goes, the Word also goes. In other words, once Jesus goes, the Bible goes after.

I live in England. On the outside of the English parliament in Westminster, London, it says *pater nostra cuis en coeleas*, 'Our Father who art in Heaven', because the British parliament was founded by Puritans who believed the Bible.

Inside, it is filled with atheists, freemasons, Muslims, and God knows what else. They certainly don't believe the Bible. Why is this society falling to bits? Why is there so much crime? Why are there saved Christians, even so-called Christian ministers, getting divorced and remarried? The salt is losing its taste. They are going away from the teachings of the Bible because they have gone away from Jesus.

They have gone away from the Word, so they go away from the Word. He is the Word; if you go away from the Bible, you have gone away from Christ. It's that simple.

Salt preserves. Even in the so-called Bible belts, the immorality, crime, and divorce among so-called Christians is staggering; even more so because it is accepted. When I was first saved, you would never have heard of a Christian getting divorced and remarried. If that happened, it either happened before they were saved, or they had an unbelieving partner who left. That was it; otherwise, it never would have happened. But now it means nothing. The biggest names are doing it! It's in the newspapers! Hal Lindsay is on his third divorce and remarriage; Amy Grant is getting divorced, etc. It doesn't mean anything any more, because the salt has lost its flavour.

Let us look even further: The grain came in two ways. You had the whole grain, and then you had the crushed grain, or grits. What is the difference between the whole grain and the crushed grain? It is all the Word of God, but it comes in two forms: When the Word of God is taught under the true anointing of the Holy Spirit, that is crushed grain. It is somebody taking the Word, crushing it up, and giving it to the people in a digestible form; that is good. But the whole grain comes first. No Bible teacher, no Christian book, will ever replace your reading of the Word of God for yourself. There is good crushed grain; there are books such as *The Pilgrim's Progress, The Screwtape Letters*, books by A. W. Tozer, and many others. There is a lot of good crushed grain; however, the whole grain comes first. No teaching, no teacher, no tape, no video, no book, and no broadcast will ever replace your prayerfully reading and studying the scriptures for yourself.

The Word is the Word; the Word of the Lord, and the Lord of the Word. He is the Word; He is the grain, which was offered in three ways: He suffered in body, in soul, and in spirit when He took our sins. That grain was consumed on a griddle, in a skillet, and in an oven.

He was anointed for burial before He was anointed for kingdom dominion. There was no Benny Hinn hairstyle, no Mercedes limousine or mansion; there was a crucified life as proof of the anointing. He brought the acceptable sacrifice to the Lord.

No honey; there was no affection at the cross. The Father turned His back on His Son for my sin. I deserved nothing but hell, yet I received the affection. Jesus took my sin so that I do not have to go to hell.

No leaven; there was no false doctrine, there was no pride, there was no sin; but there was a salt; a salt that preserves. This salty grain would preserve a society, a nation, a denomination, a church, a family, and your life and mine; salt preserves.

The whole grain and the crushed grain; that is what God has for us, and that is what God wants for us. It is here waiting, and in some cases for people, the gospel has been here their entire lives, yet it has never been accepted. However, it can be accepted even today.

Christians — watch out for too much honey. Do not withhold affection, but also do not be governed by it.

This is everything. It is wonderful to be in the countries in which we live; yet something is happening in those countries — America, Britain, etc. The biblical heritage bequeathed to us by our forefathers is diminishing rapidly. We have what is increasingly becoming no more than a cultural Christianity. People who are not truly saved yet claim to be are talking the talk without walking the walk. I have no solution, but God does. That solution is the grain. We have the problem, God has the solution.

Jonah

Before we turn to the book of Jonah, turn very briefly please to the book of Acts chapter 2.24 and 27: *"And God raised Him up again, putting an end to the agony of death, since it was impossible for Him to be held in its power."* In verse 27 we have a quote from the book of Isaiah and the Psalms, *"Because thou wilt not abandon my soul to hades, nor allow thy holy one to undergo decay."* It was impossible for death to hold Jesus in its power: it was a theological, spiritual and logical impossibility.

We are told in the book of Hebrews that Isaac was willing to sacrifice his only son — as a type of Christ — because even then he knew that God could raise his son up from the dead to fulfil his purpose. It is an example of how God puts somebody in a 'death situation', with the assurance that his resurrection power is going to be found in it. With these things in view turn with me to the book of the prophet Jonah.

> The word of the LORD came to Jonah the son of Amittai saying, "Arise, go to Nineveh the great city, and cry against it, for their wickedness has come up before Me." But Jonah rose up to flee to Tarshish from the presence of the LORD. So he went down to Joppa, found a ship which was going to Tarshish, paid the fare, and went down into it to go with them to Tarshish from the presence of the LORD. And

the LORD hurled a great wind on the sea and there was a great storm on the sea so that the ship was about to break up. Then the sailors became afraid, and every man cried to his god, and they threw the cargo which was in the ship into the sea to lighten it for them. But Jonah had gone below into the hold of the ship, lain down, and fallen sound asleep. So the captain approached him and said, "How is it that you are sleeping? Get up, call on your god. Perhaps your god will be concerned about us so that we will Jonah not perish." And each man said to his mate, "Come, let us cast lots so we may learn on whose account this calamity has struck us." So they cast lots and the lot fell on Jonah. (Now in Proverbs 16:33 it says: The lot is cast into the lap, but its every decision is from the LORD.) Then they said to him, "Tell us, now! On whose account has this calamity struck us? What is your occupation? And where do you come from? What is your country? From what people are you?" And he said to them, "I am a Hebrew, and I fear the LORD God of heaven who made the sea and the dry land." Then the men became extremely frightened and they said to him, "How could you do this?" For the men knew that he was fleeing from the presence of the LORD, because he had told them. So they said to him, "What should we do to you that the sea may become calm for us?" for the sea was becoming increasingly stormy. And he said to them, "Pick me up and throw me into the sea. Then the sea will become calm for you, for I know that on account of me this great storm has come upon you." However, the men rowed desperately to return to land but they could not, for the sea was becoming even stormier against them. Then they called on the LORD and said, "We earnestly pray, O LORD, do not let us perish on account of this man's life and do not put innocent blood on us; for Thou, O LORD, hast done as Thou hast pleased." So they picked up Jonah, threw him into the sea, and the sea stopped its raging. Then the men feared the LORD greatly, and they offered a sacrifice to the LORD and made vows. And the LORD appointed a great fish to swallow Jonah, and Jonah was in the stomach of the fish three days and three nights.

We're not told it was a whale. The Jews translate this literally as in modern Hebrew *livyathan* — Leviathan, whales are not usually indigenous to the Mediterranean, we don't know what kind of fish it was, we just assume it was a whale (strictly speaking of course a whale is a mammal not a fish — it has no gills).

Then Jonah prayed to the Lord his God from the stomach of the fish,

"I called out of my distress to the LORD, And He answered me. I cried for help from the depth of Sheol; Thou didst hear my voice. "For Thou hadst cast me into the deep, Into the heart of the seas, And the current engulfed me. All Thy breakers and billows passed over me. So I said, 'I have been expelled from Thy sight. Nevertheless I will look again toward Thy holy temple.' Water encompassed me to the point of death. The great deep engulfed me, Weeds were wrapped around my head. I descended to the roots of the mountains. The earth with its bars was around me forever, But Thou hast brought up my life from the pit, O LORD my God. While I was fainting away, I remembered the LORD; And my prayer came to Thee, Into Thy holy temple. Those who regard vain idols forsake their faithfulness, But I will sacrifice to Thee With the voice of thanksgiving. That which I have vowed I will pay. Salvation is from the LORD." Then the LORD commanded the fish, and it vomited Jonah up onto the dry land. Now the word of the LORD came to Jonah the second time, saying, "Arise, go to Nineveh the great city and proclaim to it the proclamation which I am going to tell you". So Jonah arose and went to Nineveh according to the word of the LORD. Now Nineveh was an exceedingly great city, a three days' walk. Then Jonah began to go through the city one day's walk; and he cried out and said, "Yet forty days and Nineveh will be overthrown."

Now the word here for overthrown is *nechpakeh*. It's the same word used in Genesis for the destruction of Sodom, the most terrible destruction and judgement on a city that the Jews had a record of in the Torah. By using that particular term *nechpakeh* it would have conjured visions of what God did to Sodom and Gomorrah.

Then the people of Nineveh believed in God; and they called a fast and put on sackcloth from the greatest to the least of them. When the word reached the king of Nineveh, he arose from his throne, laid aside his robe from him, covered himself with sackcloth, and sat on the ashes. And he issued a proclamation and it said, "In Nineveh by the decree of the king and his nobles: Do not let man, beast, herd, or flock taste a thing. Do not let them eat or drink water. "But both man and beast must be covered with sackcloth; and let men call on God earnestly that each may turn from his wicked way and from the violence which is in his hands. "Who knows, God may turn and relent, and withdraw His burning anger so that we shall not perish?" When God saw their deeds, that they turned from their wicked way, then God relented concerning the calamity which He had declared He would bring upon them. And He did not do it. But it greatly displeased Jonah, and he became angry. And he prayed to the LORD and said, "Please LORD, was not this what I said while I was still in my own country? Therefore, in order to forestall this I fled to Tarshish, for I knew that Thou art a gracious and compassionate God, slow to anger and abundant in lovingkindness, and one who relents concerning calamity. "Therefore now, O LORD, please take my life from me, for death is better to me than life." And the LORD said, "Do you have good reason to be angry?" Then Jonah went out from the city and sat east of it. There he made a shelter for himself and sat under it in the shade until he could see what would happen in the city. So the LORD God appointed a plant and it grew up over Jonah to be a shade over his head to deliver him from his discomfort. And Jonah was extremely happy about the plant. But God appointed a worm when dawn came the next day, and it attacked the plant and it withered. And it came about when the sun came up that God appointed a scorching east wind, and the sun beat down on Jonah's head so that he became faint and begged with all his soul to die, saying, "Death is better to me than life." Then God said to Jonah, "Do you have good reason to be angry about the plant?" And he said, "I have good reason to be angry, even to death." Then the LORD said, "You had compassion on the plant for which you did not work, and which you did not cause to grow, which came up overnight and perished overnight. "And should I not have compassion on Nineveh, the great city in which there are more than 120,000 persons who do not know the difference between their right and left hand, as well as many animals?"

Now understand that this is a very arid climate — it's not that the air conditioning isn't working — this was a gruelling situation to be in.

Now the idea of not knowing the difference between their right hand or their left hand in the Hebrew text is this: you'd have the term yad , right hand is *yemani,* as in "If I forget thee, O Jerusalem, may I forget my right hand." *Im eschcachak yerushalim tishcah yemani* (the King James mistranslates it "my right hand forget her skill" — it's not what is says in the Hebrew).

"The Lord will bring salvation with his right hand". Isaiah has the same, *"to whom has the arm —* same Hebrew word *yad — of the Lord been revealed?"* The right hand is a type of Jesus in the Old Testament. What it is basically saying is, "these pagans don't know the way of salvation, they don't know the difference between the right hand and the left

hand they don't know how to save themselves." It's the right hand of the Lord that brings salvation. That would be the implication from the Hebrew term: the right hand.

Quite a story! It was probably written during the reign of Jeroboam, somewhere between 814 and 783 BCE. We also know from history that there was an Assyrian king who became a monotheistic king, his name was Adad-Nirari III who reigned roughly from 810 to 782 (there was actually one Egyptian pharaoh who became a monotheist and there were a couple of kings of Babylon who became monotheists — see the book of Daniel). It may have been this king who turned to the true God.

Jews were always called to be lights to the gentiles — even in the Old Testament. They didn't do it the same way we do it now but if salvation was to come from the Jews, as Jesus said in John chapter four, they were still to be his witnesses to these nations and show them the true God. Today rabbis complain about "Christians" proselytising Jews, forgetting that the Jews themselves, based on what Moses originally decreed, were supposed to be out trying to win people to believe in the true God! The very fact that they are not doing that, shows that they are no longer practising a true Judaism.

Jonah was reluctant to go to Nineveh and not without good reason. These were, to say the least, not the nicest people in the world: they were 'bad people', they were total heathens! More than that, as a Bible- believing Jew, he would have read the prophecies of his predecessor the prophet Amos and he would have seen what God decreed and predicted through Amos about Nineveh. So he would even have had a biblical basis for not wanting to go there. It was not just that he knew God would have compassion on them but that they might kill him. He knew that, on the face of it, they were destined for judgement, as the prophet Nahum had predicted (and this happened at a later point when they turned back to their pagan ways), he had good reason not to go.

But let's begin with Jonah's name *'Yonah'*, meaning, in Hebrew, a dove. What images would this conjure up? One is in John 2:16. Jesus drove the people out of the temple who were selling doves (this comes from Leviticus 14. A dove was an animal deemed suitable for sacrifice and as such it was a type of Christ — as all these animals were). In the song of Solomon chapter 1:5, he tells the lover that her eyes are like doves.

Eyes because doves are monogamous birds and they only have a relationship with their partners, they don't procreate with other doves. So too in Genesis 8, first Noah sends out a bird that the Torah would later decree to be *'unkosha'* — a raven, but the second bird he sends out is a dove. All these images would have been conjured up in the minds of Jews. In the New Testament Matthew chapter 3:18, the Holy Spirit descends upon Jesus as a dove. All these images might highlight some aspect of Jonah and his character but probably the most important is found in the Psalm of David 55:4-6: *"My heart is in anguish within me, And the terrors of death have fallen upon me. Fear and trembling come upon me; And horror has overwhelmed me. And I said, "Oh, that I had wings like a dove! I would fly away and be at rest."*

The idea is this: wanting to escape from the calamity that has come upon you and Jonah was a man that wanted to escape from the calamity that came upon him!

But what about this calamity, what does it mean for us? What we have to understand about Jonah is the first thing we have to understand about all the Hebrew prophets. Every single Hebrew prophet is a type of Jesus, a type of the Messiah, every one of them foreshadows him: who he would be and what he would do. There is no Hebrew prophet whose life does not foreshadow or typify the Messiah who would come after them, to bring in the Redemption which they prophesied.

Let's look at Jonah as a type of Jesus. Turn with me please to 2 Kings chapter 14:25. That's the first place we read about Jonah in the bible.

> "He [Jeroboam] restored the border of Israel from and the entrance of Hamath as far as the sea of Havenah, according to the word of the Lord the God of Israel, which he spoke through his servant Jonah the son of Amittai the prophet who was of Gath-hepher."

Notice that Jonah was sent to his own people the Jews first — only after this was he sent to the gentiles. In Matthew chapter 15:24 we read the following: "But Jesus said, 'I was sent only to the lost sheep of the house of Israel'". Jesus was first sent only to his own people, then only at a later point was he sent to the non Jews. We are told that Jonah was from this particular area Gath-hepher: Gath-hepher is in walking distance of Nazareth.

Now there was something unique about Jonah in this. Turn with me to John chapter 7:52 — something here that the Sanhedrin overlooked! *"They answered and said to him, 'You are not also from Galilee are you? Search and see that no prophet arises out of Galilee.' "* (or as they say in the same chapter, verse 41) *"The Messiah is not going to come from Galilee, is he?"* No prophet comes from Galilee? They were wrong.

Jonah came from Galilee! He's the only one except for Jesus who was from Galilee. Jonah chapter 1:4-6, a terrible storm comes, and the word for wind in Greek in the New Testament is *pneuma* and in the Hebrew it is of course ruach , but in both it is also the word for spirit. In this storm sent by God, during the storm Jonah sleeps in the boat and the other people are frantic about this, "How can you be sleeping in the boat during the storm?"

[We have a tape on this, *The boats of the Bible* on Mark chapter 4 and 6, where we explain the typology of the boats in greater depth.] But let's look very briefly at Mark chapter 4:37-38: *"And there arose a fierce gale of wind* (same idea this would look very much like the Septuagint Greek version of Jonah), *and the waves were breaking over the boat so much that the boat was already filling up. And He Himself was in the stern, asleep on the cushion; and they awoke Him and said to Him, 'Teacher, do You not care that we are perishing?'"*

What happens to Jonah prefigures what will happen to the Lord Jesus. Jonah becomes a type of Christ. Now let's understand this a bit more. Jonah 1:12,

> **"Pick me up and throw me into the sea then the sea will become calm for you."**

Jonah, of his own choice, was willing to lay down his own life to bring salvation to others, including gentiles. John 10:17-18, *"For this reason the Father loves me because I lay down my life that I might take it again, no one is taking it from me but that I lay it down of my own initiative"*.

Jonah was willing to lay his life down to bring salvation and deliverance to others, so the Messiah, who Jonah prefigures, was willing to lay his life down so salvation would come to others. Turn with me now please to Luke chapter 11:30 *"For just as Jonah became a sign to the Israelites, so shall the son of man be to this generation."*

We know from Kings that Jonah was the son of Amittai. He

prophesied during the reigns of Jeroboam [both very bad men/kings. There were two Jeroboams; one was as bad as the other]. At the preaching of Jonah the gentiles repented when the Jews would not, at the message of Jesus the gentiles accepted what he said at a time most Jews did not. Not all Jews rejected him, not all Jews rejected Jonah. But basically, it was the gentiles not the Jews who repented in the days of Jonah and it was the gentiles not the Jews who repented in the days of Jesus. Jonah 1:17 tells us this: *"The Lord appointed a great fish"*.

The Lord sent the storm in chapter 2:1. Jonah prayed in the stomach of the fish, he said *"I called out of my distress, and he answered me, etc."*

The Lord appointed the storm, the Lord appointed the great fish. Now this was a "death experience". Some argue from the Hebrew text that Jonah may have actually died biologically, from the implications of what 'Sheol' could mean. But certainly the connotation would be there of a 'death place'. It was the Lord who appointed Jonah to a place of death, the Lord consigned him to it. In Acts chapter 2:23 we read, *"this man, delivered up by the predetermined plan and foreknowledge of God..."*

Isaiah 53:10, *"It was the will of the Lord to smite him."*

Jonah was delivered up by the foreknowledge of God to a place of destruction, Jesus was delivered up by the foreknowledge of God to a place of destruction. Jonah 'died' in the sea, he died, as it were, his death experience [whether he died or not people may debate but his death experience took place in the sea].

Turn with me please to Psalm 69. This is of course a psalm of David which is Messianic prophecy in the literary genre of Hebrew poetry. It is in this psalm for instance, we read in verse 21, *"They gave me gall for my food and they gave me vinegar to drink"*. A prophesy of what would happen when the Lord Jesus was on the cross. However, this psalm which looks ahead to the death of Jesus begins, *"Hoshanna Elohim: save me O God from the waters that have threatened my life"*. Metaphorically then the death of Jesus is represented in Hebrew prophesy as a drowning experience. Now we just sang this wonderful hymn, "When peace like a river attended my soul; when sorrows like sea billows roll", this was written by Mr Stockwood but what many people don't know and what I didn't know until five or six years ago is that he composed it after his family drowned where, of all places, a building of the American colony hotel now stands in Jerusalem. It was after his family died that he actually wrote it in Jerusalem. The idea of "sea billows roll" is the drowning experience that happened to his family — but also in biblical typology particularly the Psalms — you see, when people are under this kind of death experience, it is alluded to as drowning and points to Jesus.

Jonah chapter 3:8:

> "But both man and beast in sack cloth and ashes repented after Jonah had told these people, 'Repent, repent, repent, God will destroy this city in forty days.' And he goes on to say, 'perhaps if you repent God may turn back — (in verse 8) he may relent'".

Recently I actually had a long email from somebody trying to justify people who predict things that don't happen. He was trying to justify Rick Joyner, Gerald Coates and these guys, by saying, "Well, was Jonah a false prophet? Look at what Jonah predicted and it didn't happen." That was his argument to justify these false prophets! However, the text of Jonah makes it very clear that it was a conditional prophecy: that says "if you don't repent this is what's going to happen." He never said that it was going to happen — full stop. It was conditional. It's an unfair comparison — but they always have to pervert the Bible out of context.

Nonetheless we see that Jonah gave a direct message of 'repentance because the judgement is coming.' In the gospel of St Matthew chapter 4:17, Jesus began to preach, *"repent because the kingdom of heaven is at hand."* Jonah gave a message of repentance so that judgement could be averted, so it was with Jesus and his disciples. *"Save yourself from this wicked generation."* Jonah chapter 2:4 –

> "So I said, 'I have been expelled from thy sight from before thine eyes.'

The Hebrew says that Jonah was expelled *"from before the presence of God"*, God could not look upon him, God wouldn't look upon him, he was cast away from before God's eyes. We look at the gospel of St Matthew chapter 27:46, *"Eli Eli Lama Sabachthani — my God, my God why have you forsaken me"*. Jonah was cast away from the presence of God's sight, God would not look upon Jonah, so God would not look upon Jesus.

Jonah 1:17 He was three days and three nights in the stomach of the great fish and, as Jesus of course tells us in Matthew 17:39-40, that's a picture of the resurrection. As Jonah was three days in the stomach of the great fish, so Jesus would be three days in a tomb. Jonah is, like all of Israel's prophets, a type of Jesus. He teaches about the Messiah who would come after him, every Hebrew prophet does. When you read their lives carefully, they teach something about the Messiah — and Jonah is no exception.

Jonah is given over to this death experience, but there were things in Jonah's life that were blocking him from being conformed to what God wanted him to be.

1. He resisted God's will, he didn't want to do what God wanted him to do and again not without good reason: he knew what Amos had said about this nation that he was been sent to, he knew these people were bad. Who wants to be sent to a place like that where you might get killed?

2. Secondly, he lacked the compassion of God. He understood the judgement and anger of God but he lacked the compassion of God, and he was very good at something which we say in Yiddish: *treching*, complaining. *Trech, trech, trech*, complain, complain, complain. Somebody who with good reason doesn't want to do what God wants them to do. What God was asking him to do was very difficult: to go to a people he didn't even like, a people who were going to hate him because he wasn't one of them. In terms of the ancient world, he was from the west they were from the east.

Just by virtue of the fact that he was a Hebrew, a believer in the true God, not a pagan and that he was from the west of the known world and they were from the east, that made him a target just by going there. His complaint was not without good reason: the things he was concerned with were valid points, humanly speaking. It was difficult for him to understand how God could have such compassion on such barbarians.

You know for me it would be like, I suppose, going to fundamentalist muslims who put a bomb on a aeroplane at Lockerby, or who want to kill my Israeli family, or perhaps like a Jew being sent as a evangelist to the generation of Germans who carried out the Holocaust. There were good reasons, humanly speaking, why he could not feel or experience the compassion of God for these people, these were bad men.

It says the word of the Lord came twice to Jonah. Now the word for word in Hebrew is *davar,* but in Greek it's *Logos.* It doesn't mean a message so much as it means a person. Jesus is the Logos/davar in the Old Testament. Once more, in the Old Testament the Holy Spirit was only for certain people at certain times, high priests kings and prophets but the Holy Spirit still communicated Jesus to them the way he does us. It was only Jesus' identity that was not there but it was still him: "the word came", it means "the Lord Jesus came". It was a christological encounter with Christ in Old Testament terms. Again when Adam heard God walking in the garden — that was Jesus. When Jacob wrestled with the Metatrone (angel of God), it was Jesus. Jesus was in the Old Testament the same as in the New. When the word of the Lord came, it was a encounter with Christ.

When the Lord asks you or me to do things we don't want to do, or when there are things in my character or your character that are blocking what God wants, the Lord's not going to give you just a message, he's going to come to you. Jesus is going to stand in front of you, you're going to 'see' him. The message is going to be obvious once he comes and you'll know what's wrong with you! It's the encounter with the person, not just the word or the message or a letter or a telegram, a fax, an email — it's the person. When Jesus comes to us we'll know where we stand, when we stand in front of him.

In the Hebrew part of the world today Jews normally name their children after dead ancestors but in the Bible they named them after biblical characters in Israel's history. In Hebraic thought, 'son of', does not simply mean offspring — biological descent or pedigree, it means in the character of. Turn with me please to Matthew 16:17, Jesus said, *"Blessed are you Simon bar Jonah"* — that's of course Aramaic and not Hebrew: the Hebrew would be *ben Jonah.* Now why is Jesus calling him by his surname as well as his first name? True his father's name was Jonah but there's more to it than that: it's providential that Peter's name was Bar Jonah. He's in the character of Jonah — and so are you and so am I.

Here they go to the place Caesarea Philippi: a place where the Greeks had worshipped Pan and a place where the Romans worshipped Caesar Augustus. Here in Matthew 16:22 Peter was very angry and wanted Jesus to deal with and judge these pagan gentiles for defiling the holy land just as Jonah wanted the Lord to judge the gentiles. Jonah didn't want to go to the gentiles did he? Neither did Peter — in the character of Jonah — in Acts chapter 10, the story of Cornelius and the 'non-kosher' food, Peter did not want to go to the gentiles just as Jonah didn't. "You are Bar Jonah", "Peter, you are in the character of Jonah, you don't like these Greeks and Romans, you're in the character of Jonah, he didn't like the pagans either, you're in the character of Jonah: he didn't want to go where I wanted him to go."

Look at John 21:18: *"Truly, truly, I say to you* (he's speaking here to Peter), *when you were younger, you used to gird yourself, and walk wherever you wished; but when you grow old, you will stretch out your hands, and someone else will gird you, and bring you where you do not wish to go"*.

Peter, in the character of Jonah, didn't want to go. Look at Galatians chapter 2:11-12: Jonah had an attitude against non Jews that made him behave less than honourably, Gal 2:11: *"But when Cephas came to Antioch, I opposed him to his face, because he stood condemned. For prior to the coming of certain men from James, he used to eat with the Gentiles; but when they came, he began to withdraw and hold himself aloof, fearing the party of the circumcision."*

Jonah didn't want to get involved with these gentiles, nor did Peter bar Jonah want to get involved with gentiles! There are a lot of people I don't want to get involved with. As a younger believer I went through terrible, terrible battles of hatred and I mean hatred. I remember I saw the film The Hiding place — Corrie ten Boom and what the Nazis did to these Christians, these believers in Holland who protected Jews: how they murdered the old man and raped the women and so forth — and I was so angry. I began praising God for creating hell, not just for Nazis but for Germans — I hated Germans. When we take our tours to Israel we go to *Yad vashem* [the Holocaust Memorial] I stay in the bus. I don't go in there. I remember once I visited the Nazi death camp at Dachau where the Germans did the experiments on the Jewish children. I just think of my own children. I think even of that little girl hiding in the movie Schindler's List. I could just picture my son Eli in that situation. I battled with hatred towards Germans.

My father was in the American military in the second world war: his family was from Merseyside. His mother was from there. (She left before the war and came back after the war) When my father came with the American navy, he saw what the Germans did to Liverpool, how they destroyed everything including where his mother was from. And I had this hatred of German people. It took me a long time through the Lord bringing German people into my life — whom I love and who are believers — to lose this hatred.

There were some people who hated gypsies: "these people were crooks, they're connivers", but there was someone along the road who had the compassion of the Lord for the gypsies and now they're the fastest growing church in the United Kingdom, lives radically changed.

To take another example: I've been attacked by muslims even in England — physically attacked by gangs on Speakers' Corner for preaching the gospel — and it's not a racial thing: I love Asian Christians: they're great people. But when I read what the Muslims do in Pakistan to Christians or what they do to Christians in Saudi Arabia I get angry. I look at the Amnesty International website and I just get so angry.

One of the great blessings of my life, one of the great thrills of my life was when I spoke about Islam in Auckland, New Zealand and some Iranians, who had just come to New Zealand from Iran, Shia muslims, repented and accepted Jesus and renounced Mohammed and the Koran and became believers.

I know people who were anti-Semitic before they got saved: some crooked Jewish landlord did something to their aunt Milly thirty years ago and so they hated Jews. But after they got saved the Lord gave them a love and a burden for the Jews they couldn't explain and they couldn't even understand. There's things in us, things that are not irrational, things that have some logical basis — sometimes even an apparent biblical basis: there were reasons Jonah didn't like these people. He had read what Amos said about them, he had read what God was going to do, so it was not totally irrational, in fact it was totally rational. There were good logical reasons humanly speaking. But he could not see and understand the compassion of God. No matter how bad these people are, when the word of the Lord comes to us and we stand before Jesus, we see that no matter how bad they are (even compared to us); we're all infinitely bad compared to Jesus. You know the sort of thing:

"Single mothers on council estates be warned: you've got five kids from three different yobbos and we're having to support them. Why do I have to pay taxes and support my family? To pay for these kids. Why don't these yobbos that you pick up in the pub support their own kids? Why should I have to?" It's rational but where's the compassion of Jesus for these single mothers? When I see them on the news doing these things, throwing bottles at football games: they don't care about football, they just care about getting drunk and throwing bottles — it's tribalism. "Please beat their heads in", that's me! Not altogether irrational but where's the compassion of Jesus? I've known yobbos who've got saved, I've known muslims who've been saved and I've known prostitutes who've been saved and I've known drug addicts who've been saved: I used to be one! Where is the compassion of Jesus?

So Jonah gets plunged, God creates a storm. God appoints a death and there he finds himself buried in the guts of a fish, underneath the Mediterranean somewhere between Turkey and Tel Aviv. Now this particular experience is one of the things in the Bible which theologically teaches about life after death. But it also is one of the things that reveals something about what will happen to Jesus. When he died on the cross for our sin, when his Father couldn't look upon him, when his father's voice went into the depths of sheol and raised him from the dead. We are told in Acts 2:24 that death itself could not contain Jesus Christ, the grave was not strong enough to contain him, death itself was not strong enough to control Jesus, to hold him in.

Turn with me please to 2 Corinthians 4:8-14: *"we are afflicted in every way, but not crushed; perplexed, but not despairing; persecuted, but not forsaken; struck down, but not destroyed; always carrying about in the body the dying of Jesus, that the life of Jesus also may be manifested in our body. For we who live are constantly being delivered over to death for Jesus' sake, that the life of Jesus also may be manifested in our mortal flesh. So death works in us, but life in you. But having the same spirit of faith, according to what is written, "I believed, therefore I spoke," we also believe, therefore also we speak; knowing that He who raised the Lord Jesus will raise us also with Jesus and will present us with you."*

As the prophet Hosea puts it in chapter 6:2, the resurrection of the Lord Jesus is our resurrection because his death is our death. Look at what Hosea says, *"He will revive us after two days; and the third day he will raise us up that we may live before him"*.

Because Jesus' death is our death, his resurrection is our resurrection, could death contain Jesus? No! Can death contain you or I? Because of Jesus, No! There are no shortage of things in my life that block what God is wanting me to be, and things in my life that are blocking me from really doing what God is wanting me to do. Sometimes I feel like I am being put to death, when I complain about my neck, when I complain about being rejected by so much of the popular church because I won't go along with what's going on. Then I get a copy of Brother Andrew's newsletter and I read of Christians living in almost sub-human poverty, imprisoned and their families unable to support themselves. My kids have a roof over their head: what do I have to complain about? Yes my neck hurts but I have pills. There are people whose necks hurt and they don't have the money for a pill. I have a pill in my pocket if my neck goes into spasm, I carry it around with me. All that bothers me. Why am I being put to death?

Why is it that ministries who teach the truth are always struggling for money but the ones who are corrupt rake it in? Because they struggle for money too — only they are expanding their corruption! Honest ministries are trying to expand the truth — they have to struggle and trust God. Death works in me. Why, Lord, if I am teaching the truth? I was only upholding the Trinity yet people who were part of Moriel began using my name a few weeks ago to endorse people who denied it. When I took the stand, they slandered me, they said I was mentally unbalanced from my automobile accident. Maybe I am unbalanced — but not from my automobile accident — who needs this? What those people did was wicked but the real question is why did God allow it? What is God saying to me in this? God will deal with them but what is he saying to me? When my neck hurts the way it does today, (I am going to have to take a pill pretty soon!) what's God saying to me? What's God saying to you, when you are in the fish's guts? Remember Jesus said he's like Jonah: it seems like God himself banishes us from his presence. We are behaving in a way we think is reasonable and at least it's not irrational. We had reason on our side but we are in this bad situation. Sometimes lousy employment, sometimes no employment, financial hardship, health problems, problems in the church, problems in the ministry, problems in the family, problems in the marriage, problems, problems, problems. It seems like the Lord has banished us from his presence, he put us in a tomb, he left us in a grave. Oh! Not the Ninevites, not the Mormons or the Muslims, not the yobbos or the prostitutes! He puts us in the grave.

He's banished us from his sight. But death could not contain Jesus and death cannot contain you either. I've said a thousand times the test of a true Christian is not that they don't have trials — on the contrary if you don't have trials you're not a Christian — you have tribulation in the world. The test of a Christian is not that you don't go into the fish's guts, the test of the trial is what happens when you're inside of it.

Turn with me to Psalm 18:4-6. There are direct parallels in the Psalms to what happened to Jonah in that fish's gut. *"The cords of death encompassed me, And the torrents of ungodliness terrified me. The cords of Sheol surrounded me* (Jonah uses the word sheol). *The snares of death confronted me. In my distress I called upon the LORD, And cried to my God for help; He heard my voice out of His temple, And my cry for help before Him came into His ears."* We may have been banished from his sight but not from his ears. Psalm 42:7: *"Deep calls to deep at the sound of thy waterfalls and all breakers and waves have rolled over me"* (just like Jonah).

Psalm 116:3-9: *"The cords of death encompassed me, And the terrors of Sheol came upon me; I found distress and sorrow. Then I called upon the name of the LORD: "O LORD, I beseech Thee, save my life!" Gracious is the LORD, and righteous; Yes, our God is compassionate. The LORD preserves the simple; I was brought low, and He saved me. Return to your rest, O my soul, For the LORD has dealt bountifully with you. For Thou hast rescued my soul from death, My eyes from tears, My feet from stumbling. I shall walk before the LORD in the land of the living* — *not the dead."*

Even if you die there is a resurrection, there is a millennial kingdom. (Verse 15) Precious in the sight of the Lord is the death of his godly ones. Even if we die we see him not in the land of the dead but in the land of the living. What does Job say? Job 19:25-27: *"And as for me, I know that my Redeemer lives, And at the last He will take His stand on the earth. Even after my skin is destroyed, Yet from my flesh I shall see God; Whom I myself shall behold, And whom my eyes shall see and not another."* Even if we die we will see the goodness of the Lord in the land of the living.

"Out of the depths I cry to thee O Lord", wrote David. When you're in the depths, you've been banished from God's own presence. Your arguments are rational — at least to your own mind, certainly they are

logical and even to a degree biblical. There you are in the stomach of the fish, the waves have overtaken you, you are not only drowning but are perhaps drowned. The bars of sheol give you no way out and you can't even see the Lord: he has banished you from his presence. But these Psalms don't tell us he looks upon us, they say he hears. Then and only then did the fish regurgitate Jonah out onto the beach. He must have looked a mess and smelt even worse but he was ready for action! When you go through a mess like this you might not look so good either and could also do with a bottle of eau de cologne, but you'll be ready for action. As Paul said, his death is our death, so his resurrection our resurrection.

Death could not contain him, death cannot contain us. As Hosea said, his death is our death, his resurrection our resurrection, death could not contain Jesus and death cannot contain us. You're going down for the third time, you're in the gut of the world. God is calling you to do things you don't want to do, you know there's things in your life and in your character that don't reflect the character of Jesus. Like Peter you are bar Jonah. Like Peter I am bar Jonah.

Here comes the storm, the tempest that God himself sends and the fish is waiting for his lunch and it's you! There you are down in the depths, banished before the eyes of God himself, while the wicked continue in their wickedness, instead of setting his hand against them he has set it against you. You've had it spiritually, you've had it emotionally.

"For Thou hadst cast me into the deep, Into the heart of the seas, And the current engulfed me. All Thy breakers and billows passed over me. So I said, 'I have been expelled from Thy sight. Nevertheless I will look again toward Thy holy temple.' Water encompassed me to the point of death. The great deep engulfed me, Weeds were wrapped around my head. I descended to the roots of the mountains. The earth with its bars was around me forever, But Thou hast brought up my life from the pit, O LORD my God. While I was fainting away, I remembered the LORD; And my prayer came to Thee, into Thy holy temple. Those who regard vain idols forsake their faithfulness, But I will sacrifice to Thee with the voice of thanksgiving. That which I have vowed I will pay. Salvation is from the LORD."

When I was born again I made a vow. I vowed that I would accept Jesus as the Lord of my life, the one who saved me; he gave his life to me, I vowed I'd give my life to him. Every time I fall into sin I am not keeping that vow, every time I resist His will I am not keeping that vow. I made the vow but when it comes time to pay up I can always find a very logical argument, not infrequently even a scriptural argument, against 'paying up'! When you make a vow to the Lord don't delay in paying it, he won't let you out of it. The storm will come, the fish will eat you, but the fish couldn't hold Jonah and it won't hold you either, the grave couldn't hold Jesus and it won't hold you either. You tell the Lord you'll pay that vow.

You know, what has happened to you has happened for a reason, the fish will vomit you out on the beach as well. I think every one of us should be called bar Jonah. I certainly think it's a name that suits me: bar Jonah. It says "the billows and waves overtook me." Sometimes the billows and waves overtake me and even though it may be the people, what is God saying in it? I don't know what he is saying to you, sometimes I am not even clear what he is saying to me but I know this, sometimes the only place you're ever going to find out is in the gut of the fish. This fish could not devour Jonah, the grave couldn't hold Christ. The fish could not devour Jonah, he was invincible no matter what it seemed like. No matter how adverse the circumstances, even out of God's sight that fish could not hold him, that grave could not hold Jesus Christ. I don't know what fish swallowed you, I don't know what tomb you might be in but it can't hold you either.

God bless you.

Once Christian Marriage Means Nothing

From around the world in recent months, Moriel has experienced something of a minor flood of emails, post, and calls about the divorce, and often remarriage of various high profile preachers. This has not simply included the divorces and remarriages themselves, but also other prominent preachers going along with it, almost pretending that nothing happened, as if the biblical permanency and sanctity of holy wedlock no longer mattered in the Body of Christ any more than it does in secular post Judeo-Christian society.

We have, in our teaching tapes, often pointed out that as the first kind of fellowship God ordained (apart from Adam's communion with Him) was marriage, it is in God's blueprint for the human race the foundation of society.

Once the foundation cracks, society cracks. Thus we see a direct proportional relationship between children from broken homes and single parent families and juvenile delinquency.

More fundamentally still, marriage represented the essence of *Imagio Dei*; that man was made in the image and likeness of his triune creator. The same as the constituency of our being is tripartite in terms of having a body, a soul, and a spirit, so the marital union was to reflect this. The Hebrew term for the eternal oneness of God *Achad* in the *Shma* (the Hebrew confession of faith which Jesus called the greatest commandment) "The Lord your God is One" is better translated 'Oneness' designating a plural oneness. As we are made in His image, because He loves — He designs us to want to love and to be loved. Because He is creative, making us in His image. Not least of all however, because His Once Christian marriage means nothing own divine unity within the Godhead is permanent, He designed marriage accordingly as something He joined together that "no man should put asunder".

Thus the Hebrew term for marital sex in the scriptures is generally *niknas ba*, literally "to go into her" where a bond is to be formed, designed to permanently seal two souls together via an act of physical oneness. Thus, in marital intimacy, one person is inside of another person and a third person is procreated. We have one in three, and three in one. This somehow, howbeit mysteriously, reflects something of the Trinity in whose image we are created. While designed by the Creator to be erotically pleasurable, there is a spiritual dimension to marital romance transcending physical and emotional gratification, passionate intimacy, and the procreation of children. It is a bonding agent; a cement intended to last as long as temporal life does.

Yet even this falls well short of a scriptural understanding of marriage. The union was to be physical, psychological (as in emotional and intellectual), and because it is based on a mutual vow made to God, spiritual. The horizontal relationship with its physical, psychological, emotional, social, and legal links was to be predicated on a shared vertical relationship with God sealed with a solemn vow to Him as the basis of marriage. Sadly blind as they are to the messiahship of Yeshua, Orthodox Jews have some grasp of these concepts, mystically believing the Shekinah hovers over the marriage bed and that Israel's covenant relationship with God has a counterpart in the *Ketubah*, a kind of ceremonial marriage contract carrying weight in *halakik* Jewish religious law.

As with so much of the talmudic Judaism invented by the rabbis to replace the biblical Judaism of the Torah fulfilled in the Messiah, otherwise valid truths are reinterpreted in light of kabbalistic mysticism, but the basic concept itself has a fair amount of biblical merit.

Once we contemplate how marriage, sexual intimacy, and procreation mirror things divine and constitute the foundations of God's idea of society, the manner in which divorce and remarriage undermine His designs becomes obvious.

The biblical theology of marriage however, while certainly inclusive of romance and sexuality (for this we would recommend Dr Arnold Fruchtenbaum's commentary on The Song of Songs), in actual fact goes well beyond it.

Thus even the erroneous talmudic Judaism of the rabbis realises that holy matrimony is the reflected image of the divine relationship with Israel (Hosea 2:7 — where the word for husband is *ish* meaning "her personal 'man'", Jeremiah 3;20 — where the word is *rea*, meaning "her 'intimate friend'" and Jeremiah 31:32 — where the word is *baal*, literally "the one who possesses her"; as in a husband and a wife sexually "possess" each other's body as in 1 Corinthians 7:4, so our bodies — the Greek word Soma — are for the Lord in 1 Corinthians 6:13). These three terms indicate primary aspects of what Israel's relationship with God was to be like, and that akin to what a marital relationship was to be like. The term used in the Hebrew nuptial ritual for "to wed" is *mekudeshet*, meaning the husband "sanctifies" his wife in God's sight making the union holy by a divine "setting apart". This is essentially the same term used for the consecration of the High Priest to make atonement, and theologically is a very serious and heavy term never used lightly.

The difference was that in those days it was the unfaithful bride (Israel) who departed from her husband, the husband refused to depart. Today, Christian husbands and even preachers are often the ones doing the departing.

Even after a bill of divorce became necessary due to the unrepentant *znut* or harlotry which was the metaphor for idol worship (Jeremiah 3:8) and God said *Lo Ammi* ("not my people" — Hosea 1:9), He immediately claims that despite her infidelity He would reclaim her after dealing with her sin (Hosea 2:1-7). God proclaims that there is no bill of divorce, and that no man can put the relationship asunder (Isaiah:50:1-2). Despite the false doctrines of replacement theology, the "so called Christian" anti Zionism of Rick Godwin and the

Restorationists, and the anti-Semitic lies of the Identity Movement who influence the likes of W.B. Howard and W. Buester, the Lord promises and predicts He would again turn His grace back to Israel in His eschatological calendar (Isaiah 66:20-24, Romans 11:25-27, Isaiah 59:20, Revelation 7:4-8).

It is therefore perhaps little coincidence that promoters of Godwin's so-called ministry which teaches God has put his relationship with Israel asunder, such as Ray Bevin in South Wales and Ray Macauley in South Africa, are the very ones whose own marriages get put asunder. Macauley has just split with his wife against the background of the cricket bribe scandal involving leading members of his church. A public scandal has rocked Bevin's Welsh church after he divorced his wife to marry another woman and front page newspaper articles are virtually labelling his church a cult on the testimony of those who have left it feeling like victims of exploitation. Bevin's church said they have no fixed policy on divorce and remarriage. While Bevin may not have a policy on divorce, God however does — He hates it, and those not hating it do not take heed of their spirit and they are treacherous (Malachi 2:16).

Similarly, it is of very little surprise that in the UK, the Elim denomination is advertising a conference of Macaulley where he is to be joined by Elim's elder statesman George Canty, who teaches that "Jesus Christ had no Jewish blood".

These same principles of God's divine marriage with Israel apply to and are replayed and expanded in Christ's relationship with His bride the believing church (Revelation 21:2). Concerning Mr Canty's Elim movement, we actually have a copy of a letter from Elim's recently retired honcho Wynn Lewis to a Pentecostal leader in Texas in which, while not trying to defend the act, Lewis attempts to downplay the seriousness of an Elim minister sent to prison for having sex with a minor in an Elim church because the girl was 15.

This conference Elim is pushing in Birmingham is of all things called "Fire". The cast of characters speaking at that thing may be leading people into the fire alright, but not the fire of the Holy Spirit. We do see a connection between the false belief that God permanently divorced Israel, and those holding such views getting divorced and remarried.

So too, sexual oneness has its parody in oneness with Christ, and that our bodies too are not as such our own but are owned (1 Corinthians 6:16-20). Once more, Christian marriage reflects Christ's marriage to the church (Ephesians 5:23-25). The romance and the longing of the ancient Hebrew betrothal in anticipation of the nuptial portrays the church waiting for the return of Jesus (Matthew 25:1-13, Song of Songs 3:1-5, 7:1—8:14).

Thus, the New Testament plainly outlaws divorce unless one has an unbelieving spouse who abandons the believer, or a partner is involved in unrepentant adultery (Matthew 5:32, 1 Corinthians 7:15). Fifteen years ago, the only cases where a Christian was divorced is if it happened before they were saved Christians, an unbelieving spouse abandoned them or was involved in an adulterous affair, or their was a spouse backslidden into adultery who would not repent and became as a non-believer (1 Corinthians 5:13, Matthew 18: 17).

Today, it is different. Now leading preachers who have no right whatsoever to even be in the ministry are with broken marriages (1 Timothy 3:4-5, Titus 1:6). Today however, among others, Richard Roberts, the hyper charismatic son of money preacher Oral Roberts is divorced as a supposed Christian and remarried, yet still has a TV following on the heretical TBN. Hal Lindsay, author of "Late Great Planet Earth" is similarly on the TBN, while he is presently on his third marriage (which is why Moriel will not carry his books). Likewise, Peter Ruckman, godfather of the King James Only Movement, is also divorced and remarried three times.

Again, when one comprehends how Satan is trying to dismantle society and prevent the image and likeness of God being reflected on the earth, one automatically grasps the strategy underlying promiscuity, homosexuality, same sex marriages with legal rights to artificially inseminate and/or adopt, and of course a fifty percent divorce rate. The church of Jesus Christ however is called by Him to be the obvious alternative to this. Instead Anglicans, Methodists, Reformed churches and the Lord knows who else are ordaining homosexuals (something neither Islam nor Mormonism would even do; cults and Islam have higher moral standards than the most visible Protestant churches). Homosexual and lesbian clergy met in an Anglican Cathedrals in London and the homosexual dean of the Anglican Cathedral in Cape Town appearing on TV dressed in Anglican vestments actually sporting a devil's tail promoting homosexuality, while other Anglicans caught up in deception, gimmicks, and hype artistry claim there is revival.

But divorce is as much a component of Satan's assault on the family as is homosexuality. So instead of the evangelical Christian church maintaining a witness and testimony for Christ and being salt and light in society with stable committed marriages, divorce among Christians now abounds and the salt is good for nothing but to be trampled on the ground courtesy of men like Ray Bevin, Peter Horrobin, and Peter Ruckman.

Thanks not only to them, but to those who will stand by them and join with them in so called ministry instead of disassociating from them in the prayerful hope they will repent, the only victory becomes Satan's.

The gospel believing church should be an example to a divorce ridden society of the permanency of holy matrimony, and our preachers should be examples of this to the true church. Instead, we have the opposite happening and it is accepted often in the name of love and unity. Such love however is not biblically the love of Jesus, neither is it the unity of the Spirit! Christ plainly calls such divorce and remarriage nothing less than immoral adultery (Matthew 5:32).

It should not even be found among saved Christians. No matter what our marital struggles, divorce is not an option for us, it is for the world that is going to hell.

We have had multiple complaints about Johannas Facius and The Ebenezer Fund bringing Peter Horrobin onto its board with Eliahu Ben Hayim. They are to be joined by Lance Lambert and Derek Prince at a July marathon in Bournemouth, England supposedly to "bless Israel". We will allow Steve Lightel, also at the conference, to explain why he has been away from the ministry so long, but it is the devil who wishes to sabotage the prophetic purposes of God for Israel and the Jews, and Satan will achieve this with two things: false doctrine and immorality.

Mr Horrobin, director of an institution with extreme doctrinal positions on deliverance and demonology founded in collusion with New Zealand's ecumenical Toronto advocate Bill Subritsky. We are moderately charismatic and Pentecostal ourselves in the biblical sense of those terms, but the beliefs and practices of Horrobin are void of biblical foundation, going well beyond the bounds of anything the

Word of God teaches about dealing with demons.

More seriously however, Mr Horrobin abandoned his dear wife, divorced her, and married a younger woman. While there was no evidence of any adultery at all, Mr Horrobin reportedly accused her of "spiritual adultery", which also has absolutely no biblical basis whatsoever (apart from the limited context of ancient Israel's idolatry and worldliness in the church in James 4:4, which even here has nothing to do with Christians getting divorced and remarried). The only adultery according to the New Testament would be Mr Horrobin's, and if he was going to cast a demon out of somebody, perhaps he should begin with himself.

I am indeed disgusted and ashamed that such divorce and remarriage takes place within what is supposed to be the Body of Christ. I am additionally appalled that it has infiltrated into what is supposed to be God's End Times purposes for the Jews. But most of all I am in agreement with those who writing us who are completely and utterly revolted with once respected figures like Lance Lambert and Derek Prince joining forces with it in direct rejection of the clear teaching of the Jesus Christ to whom they will one day give account.

God hates divorce, and a true Christian will always not only love what God loves, but because they love the Lord, will also hate what God hates, including so called preachers dumping their wives like a sack of rubbish and taking off with another one. Paul writes that we should not associate with such immoral so called brothers (1 Corinthians 5:9). Jesus' teaching is that divorce and remarriage are adultery, and those not abiding in his teaching are not even to be greeted. For if we do as much as greet them we participate in their evil deeds (2 John: 9-11).

Not only do Johannas Facius, Derek Prince, and Lance Lambert greet such a one, but Ebenezer promotes him to their board and they all join on a platform in co-ministry with him. This is not guilt by association, but guilt by cooperation. The word of God, not Moriel, says that they participate in his evil deeds.

Moreover, this says to the followers of Derek Prince and Lance Lambert "See, divorce and remarriage must be alright because Peter Horrobin did it and Lance Lambert and Derek Prince cominister with him". God however says, that by participating with him, Derek Prince, Johannas Facius, and Lance Lambert have participated in his sin, and as these men purport to be teachers, they will be judged even more strictly than others for doing so, as they wilfully chose to allow themselves to be used by Satan to mislead others by giving credibility to a man who did something so terrible (James 3:1).

Compromising with something God calls wrong by ignoring it and acting as if it did not happen is known in scripture as "winking the eye" at sin, (Proverbs 10:10) and the Bible says: *"they cause trouble, they bring sorrow and they become babbling fools who eventually will come to ruination"*.

Tragically, I have a dear friend and close brother whom I personally both like and appreciate very much. Yet while otherwise one of the finest preachers in England, he is caught up in unbiblical extremes of deliverance ministry and similarly to that end compromises and gets involved with Peter Horrobin, to the dismay and sometimes chagrin of many who love and esteem this brother as much as I do. I am not alone in being perplexed how such a gifted and intelligent brother can be so blind and undiscerning in one area when his perception is so astute and discernment so acute in other areas. It makes me wonder what blind spots there are in my own life and ministry. Very sadly, this brother is always battling an almost inexplicable demonic attack on himself and his much needed ministry. While attacks themselves are normal and to be expected (1 Peter 4:12), the toll these extract from him and his ministry, at times putting him out of commission, is not normal. It is the kind of thing that can drag even a solid believer into spiritual and psychological doldrums and left unresolved can result in demonic oppression and possibly even clinical depression. Indeed, at times it appears to be ruining him and his ministry. Winking the eye always does.

Thomas Moore is not the best example of someone who refused to compromise over illicit divorce in order to please man and paid with his life, because Moore's real problem was not the divorce of Henry VIII, but merely that for political considerations the Pope would not give Henry a papal dispensation to do it. Moore was as much the victim of his own misplaced loyalties as he was the axe of King Henry. Yet the divorce and remarriage were improper, Thomas Moore did oppose it, and he was consequently decapitated at the Tower of London.

A better example would be John the Baptist who would not

approve the improper remarriage of a woman to Herod and was likewise beheaded. These men refused to "wink the eye" and lost their heads. Men like Derek Prince, Eliahu Ben Hayim, Johannas Facius, and Lance Lambert, in a manner of speaking, appear to have lost their heads and then winked the eye. The thought that others faced the chopping block rather than compromise with what Lance Lambert and Derek Prince have no trouble casually aligning themselves with is a sad indictment of the current state of the church and those who pose as its leaders. When those led astray by the wrong example and flawed leadership of such eye winkers participate, financially or otherwise, in something with which Mr Horrobin is involved, on the basis of 2 John 9-11, they too partake in the sin. But why should an adulterous church be expected to care about adultery?

We have often noted that wrong doctrine invariably begets wrong conduct. As we note on our "Sons of Zadok" tape and video, the Hebrew term for being right and for being righteous is identical (tsodek), and one scripturally in God's sight cannot be a righteous person (*tsadek*) if what they believe is not correct (*tsodek*).

The idiotic notion that one can be in serious doctrinal error and still be regarded as "a good brother" is simply a nonsensical and contra-biblical invention of carnal Christianity. Being right in one's doctrine may not always guarantee that one is righteous, but being wrong certainly guarantees that they are not.

This is why the New Testament contains twice as much exhortation to right doctrine as it does right conduct; without right doctrine, we cannot know what true right conduct is. This is also why in Paul's listing of the armour in Ephesians 6, he places truth before the breastplate of righteousness in the chronological order of how the armour was to be put on. A legionnaire could not put on his breastplate without first girding his loins. So too, we cannot spiritually put on the righteousness of Jesus without first having right essential doctrine.

I recently had an encounter with what I can only describe as a pseudo spiritual woman involved with Ebenezer Trust in London. Her complaint was "let God judge", but she concretely refused to deal with the doctrinal or moral issues involved. Her words were the foolish babbling of an eye winker who is party to wickedness. God already has judged in His Word. He has directly told us what to do when there is unrepentant sin, and He has already given us His judgement about divorce and remarriage, and He commands us to act upon His judgement.

She is in rebellion against the Lord and has rejected His Word. Her only saving grace may be that she does so under the influence of the example of Derek Prince and Lance Lambert; after all she reckons "if such deeply spiritual men ignore the Word of God, it must be alright", with no reference in her thinking to what the Word of God says, nor with any regard for the victim — the abandoned wife.

As Isaiah said, Mr Facius, Mr Lambert, and Mr Prince may have their festival while accommodating what God calls open sin, and such leaders may ignore God's standards found in the Bible and persuade naîve and undiscerning Christians to believe its alright. But as Isaiah also blasted, God hates the festivals, (Isaiah 1:14-15) and such leaders misguiding people and failing to uphold God's standards are, in the Lord's eyes, but rebels (Isaiah 1:23). Giving platform and position to a man who gets rid of his wife and marries one younger may have a lot to do with Ebenezer Fund, but it has nothing to do with the actual purposes of God for his people Israel, and nothing to do with God's plan for His church.

Biblically, wrong doctrine inevitably brings wrong practice. Examining the wrong doctrines of those associated with Ebenezer Fund demonstrates the inevitable gravitation from wrong doctrine into wrong practice. Once the doctrinal standards go, the moral standards follow.

Ebenezer fund rejected warnings of scripture that God would require the blood of eternally lost Jews not warned to repent and accept the gospel (Acts 20:26-27, also Ezekiel 3: 20). Biblically, a love for the Jews (or for anyone else) that intentionally withholds the gospel of Jesus and allows them to continue on their way into eternal hell without their Messiah Jesus, cannot be the love of Jesus.

Yet Ebenezer actually signed an agreement with the Jewish authorities not to present Jesus to Jews they repatriate to Israel. Some other organisations bringing Jews to Israel do give them the gospel, but unlike Ebenezer are low key and do not try to make a "look at us" big fuss of it, they just get on with it without the hype-artistry and fanfare and do not seek the co-operation of the Jewish Agency at the expense of the gospel. As David Brickner, International Director of

Jews For Jesus wrote: "Genuine Christian Zionists are unrepentant evangelists to the Jews, these others are frauds and phonies".

There are many doctrinal errors underlying Ebenezer, including the denial by the late Gustav Schuller we have in a letter from him, denying the Bible's teaching about the Great Tribulation and the Time of Jacob's Trouble. For a Judeo Christian perspective of this Moriel recommends the work of Dr Arnold Fruchtenbaum. The Bible teaches that in this End Times calamity coming upon Israel in an eschatological recapitulation of the horrific events of 70AD predicted by Daniel and Jesus and recorded by Josephus and Eusebius, Jesus returns after two thirds of them are wiped out (Zecheriah 12-13, Luke 21:23-31). Jews are not being re- gathered for a blessing, but for the great tribulation. The blessing depends on coming to their rejected Messiah who has never rejected them (Matthew 23:39).

Ebenezer appears to have been less than forthright about its having signed this anti-Jewish evangelism agreement in its fund raising. Indeed, in the promotional literature for the July conference Mr Facius says the purpose will be to fulfil Romans Chapters 9-1 1 and the Great Commission.

Romans 9-11 itself however states that Paul's desire is that the Jews will be saved (Romans 10:1), but with no preacher, how shall they hear the gospel (Romans 10:14)? As Israeli evangelist Yacov Damkani points out on his tape, (just as the late Dr Martin Lloyd Jones pointed out on his Romans 9-11 tape series), the theme and focus of these entire three chapters regarding Israel's prophetic destiny relative to the church, read in context, is Israel being evangelised and the future of the church being prophetically bound up with and eschatologically dependent upon it.

Among other examples, Old Testament predictions of Gentiles bringing Jews back to Israel were fulfilled by the UN re-establishment of Israel, the Philo-Semitic benevolence of certain Turkish Pashas during the First Aliyeh, and Operation Moses funded by the US government — all with no help from Ebenezer. The Jewish Agency today will return any Jew to Israel without help from Christians, unless of course they believe Yeshua is the Messiah. At the same moment as Ebenezer Trust tries to bring Russian Jews to Israel without giving them the gospel, Natoly Sharanky is trying to push a law through the Israeli parliament, the Knesset, to have Jewish believers in Jesus in

Israel deported back to Russia! In this light, the entire scenario surrounding Ebenezer Trust is not only unbiblical, but ridiculous. Biblical prophecy is a sign to be recognised when it happens, biblical command is a directive to be implemented by the church. Prediction is prediction and command is command.

We are not even commanded in the Old Testament to repatriate the Jews at the cost of not preaching the gospel. On the contrary, in the literary prologue of the poetic exhortation of the Servant Songs of Isaiah commencing in chapter 40 to "Comfort Ye My People", the text plainly says we are to comfort them with the gospel (Hebrew term *besor* — Isaiah 40:9 & 52:7).

Neither are we ever commanded in the New Testament to fulfil these prophecies, but rather to give the Jews the gospel. Some organisations (with whom we have no quarrel) do both. The ludicrous notion that some are called to a social Zionist agenda void of the gospel while others to the gospel is stupid nonsense without any biblical exegetical foundation. So too is the abject claim that some witness by their words while others with their deeds. This is not biblical. We are not all evangelists, but we are all witnesses called to verbally bear witness one on one. This is the meaning of both the Greek term *martyrio* and Hebrew term *L ha Ade*. Biblically, we witness with our words and our deeds.

The very passage Mr Facius sites in his promotional literature states directly that "faith cometh by hearing the Word of Christ", but without a preacher how shall they (in the context, Israel) hear it"? (Romans 10:14- 17). His own literature indicts him and condemns his actions.

It was Christian anti-Semites who twisted the Bible this way substituting prediction for command. They read the predictions of Jews being slaughtered by gentiles in Leviticus 26 and Deuteronomy 28 and made it their business to go out and be sure the prophecy was fulfilled! Ebenezer has the same distorted hermeneutic approach to the Bible. Anti-Semites murder Jews. By sending them to hell without the gospel, Ebenezer murders them spiritually. But in both cases, unless there is a genuine repentance, God will surely require their blood!

Thus Romans 9-11, the purpose of the conference, is about the diametric opposite of what the conference was about, evangelising Jews, not refusing to.

The "Great Commission" also mentioned in the advert by Mr Facius as the focus of the conference moreover, is precisely to preach the gospel. How can Mr Facius and Ebenezer hold a conference with Derek Prince, Peter Horrobin, Eliahu Ben Hayim, and Lance Lambert and raise funds to fulfil the Great Commission and Romans 9-11 after signing an agreement promising not to do so? To say this is unethical is an understatement. If a secular charity was perceived to be raising funds under false pretences for something they will not do, the Serious Fraud Office and Charities Commission would investigate and the trustees would face the definite possibility of a fine and jail. As with Islam and cults not ordaining homosexuals, once more the world seems to have ethical and moral higher standards than the church! With this kind of misleading fund raising going on, what is a little marital immorality in addition to such men?

Mr Facius is not the only participant whose wrong doctrine has now led him into moral compromise however. Mr Lambert joined forces with Mahesh Chavada who proclaims Christians not following the laughing and being drunk experience are "wicked witches". Ironically, this group included many of Mr Lambert's own followers, most of whom were non Toronto charismatic moderates, now branded witches by his colleague. Is it therefore in any sense astounding that he has no reservations about teaming up with a preacher who dumps his Christian wife and marries another woman? Once a man like Mr Lambert betrays his own followers, teaming up with someone who denounces them as "witches", for not buying into a demonically inspired counterfeit revival, who can be perplexed that he betrays upholding the sanctity of Christian marriage by teaming up with a man like Peter Horrobin? Once the Bible goes, morals go.

Mr Lambert's joint venture with Mahesh Chavada represented a shift in his ministry and marked something of a departure from a strong biblical stance by "Prayer For Israel", Mr Lambert's sponsor who supported him in it, and is now influenced by the unbiblical beliefs of the Barnabas Movement. However sad, it is no coincidence that Chrissy Rogers and other Bible-based Christian Zionists are now leaving "Prayer For Israel" (PFI) on something less than amicable terms.

The pattern with Derek Prince unfortunately similar. Among a host of other issues, Derek Prince flatly endorsed the Pensacola deception (the American version of the Toronto Experience). The financial scandals, corrupted doctrines, open lying about the vibrating girl, and perverse antics on the Pensacola videos are perhaps best described as "sick". But as the heavy shepherding movement once did, Pensacola enjoyed the explicit sanction of Derek Prince. His doctrine on a host of issues including ecumenism is compromised, why therefore should not his moral standards be compromised?

Because there has already been a departure from sound doctrine (1 Timothy 4:6 & 13-16), the departure from moral integrity on the divorce and remarriage issue is to be anticipated. All bad practice comes from abandoning good doctrine (1 Timothy 1:10). When doctrinal integrity goes, moral integrity cannot but also go. To those writing us who are distraught about this conference and confused by the involvement of Lance Lambert and Derek Prince with this "preacher" who left a believing wife and re-married, we are saying that while we share their disappointment at the actions of these men, in light of what the Bible says about those compromising doctrine, we are frankly not at all surprised.

If Mr Prince, Mr Lambert, or Mr Facius wish to confront me in the presence of an open Christian meeting and in front of a video camera and debate these doctrinal and moral issues, I would earnestly welcome the challenge.141

How can Western post Christian, neo pagan society not morally collapse when its church compromises the moral standards of God on something as fundamental as holy wedlock? But can what is supposed to be the church of Jesus Christ not compromise when it is its own leaders who are called to be examples to others who are the very ones doing the divorces and remarriages?

Once Christian marriages are sacrificed on the altar of self will or just plain lust, with an abrogation of vows made to God, Christianity sacrifices itself to the world from whom it is no longer any visibly different, and in some cases worse. Once leaders are the high priests carrying out the sacrifice however, while other leaders by their actions and silence condone it, we have another kind of marriage. This is the unholy wedlock of doctrinal death to moral death with backsliding preachers performing the ceremony. When the church has leaders who will sign agreements not to proclaim Christ and wink the eye at a sin God hates, it has no real leaders, only theocratic politicians who like standing in pulpits masquerading as leaders. Are Lance Lambert, or Johannas Facius leaders by any biblical definition? Their declared actions publicly demonstrated categorically prove that they most certainly are not. Again, God hates divorce.

Can anyone imagine a Paul or a Peter signing an agreement to withhold the gospel from Jewish souls, or going along with divorce and remarriage in the church? If such Ebenezer Trust people really loved the Church, the Jews, and the Lord as Peter and Paul did, they would follow the commandments of the Lord as Peter and Paul did, giving no place to marital sin in the church and proclaim the gospel to Israel. But they will not, therefore they really do not love. Jesus said, "If you love me keep my commandments".

When the church of Jesus Christ under the leadership of such figures accommodates divorce and remarriage, it is no longer upholding the true teachings of Jesus, therefore biblically they cannot be upholding the true Jesus (John 14:15). Thus, it is no wonder that the same organisation refuses to preach Him to His own people who are headed for an eternal hell without Him.

Ebenezer literally means "Rock of Help". Whatever rock their help may be, the rock certainly isn't the rock whom they signed an agreement not to preach — it can't possibly be "Christ the Rock". HE HATES DIVORCE!

Show Me...

Doubting Thomas

"When, therefore, it was evening on that day, the first day of the week, and when the doors were shut where the disciples were for fear of the Jews, Jesus came and stood in their midst. And He said to them, 'Peace be with you,' and when He had said this, He showed Himself, both His hands and His side; and the disciples therefore rejoiced that they saw the Lord.

And Jesus therefore said to them, 'Peace be with you; as the Father has sent Me, I also send you'. And when He had said this, He breathed on them and He said, 'Receive the Holy Spirit. If you forgive the sins of any, their sins have been forgiven them, and if you retain the sins of any, their sins have been retained'.

But Thomas, one of the twelve, called Didymus, was not with them when Jesus came. And the other disciples were therefore saying to him, 'We have seen the Lord!', but he said to them, 'Unless I see in His hands the imprint of the nails, and put my finger into the place of the nails, and put my hand into His side, I will not believe'.

And after eight days again, His disciples were inside, and Thomas with them. And Jesus came, the doors having been shut, and stood in their midst and said, 'Peace be with you'. Then He said to Thomas, 'Reach here your finger, and see My hands; and reach here your hand and put it into My side; and be not unbelieving, but believing'. [The verse now that the Jehovah's Witnesses do not like—] Thomas answered and said to Him, 'My Lord and my God!' And Jesus said to him, 'Because you have seen Me, have you believed? Blessed are they that have not seen, and have believed'.

Many are the signs, therefore, that Jesus also performed in the presence of His disciples which are not written in this book; but these have been written that you might believe that Jesus is the Messiah, the Son of God, and that, believing, you might have life in His name."

—John 20:19-31

Show me! Let me see! Show me! Thomas was not there. Jesus' body and His resurrection teach about what our bodies will be like in the resurrection. His resurrection is our resurrection. During the millennial reign of Jesus, there will be two kinds of people on the earth: there will be those who are resurrected, or were raptured, and reign with Christ; and then there will be those people who are born during the millennium. The bodies of the ones who are born during the millennium will be slightly different — they'll be like the bodies of antediluvian man; the way people were before the flood. Just as people lived to be hundreds of years old before the flood, so they will during the millennium. People born during the millennial reign of Jesus will actually live to be centuries old. When someone dies at the age of 120, Isaiah tells us, it will be like a paediatric fatality; it will be like crib death. People will actually live, as Methuselah did, to be hundreds of years old.

The others, however, will be like Jesus. His body was recognisable, but not at first. He was able to do things such as walk through walls, etc. One of the reasons we see Him eating with the disciples after He rose from the dead is that the Holy Spirit knew that later there would be heretics who would come, denying that the resurrection of Jesus was literal and physical. In the ancient church, they were called Docetists, but today they are the Jehovah's Witnesses. They deny that the resurrection actually happened. That is why, in the New Testament, whenever you see someone being raised from the dead you always see Jesus eating with them, or you see them being instructed to eat. When He raised the little girl from the dead, he instructed her parents to give her something to eat. When Jesus raised Lazarus from the dead, He eats with him immediately after that in

John 12. Spiritual bodies do not need to eat; physical ones do. This testifies that the resurrection was literal.

But Thomas wasn't there; and he says, "Show me. You want me to believe in Jesus, show me. Let me see this body that was crucified, and is now alive". Thomas is what theologians would call a corporate solidarity. Corporate solidarity is the term for when one person represents a larger group of people; when one person is a sort of spiritual picture of a larger group of people. Thomas is a corporate solidarity, and he represents three different kinds of people:

The first group of people which Thomas, the twin, called Didymus, represents is his fellow Jews. He says, *"I will not believe that Jesus rose from the dead until I see the wounds in His hands"*. Look at the book of Zechariah chapter 12. In it we are told this: when Jesus comes back in the last days of the Great Tribulation, in verse 10 of chapter 12, *"I will pour out on the house of David and on the inhabitants of Jerusalem the Spirit of grace and supplication. So they will look upon Me whom they have pierced, and mourn for Him as one mourns for an only son, and weep bitterly over Him like the bitter weeping over a firstborn."*

In the great tribulation at the end, the Jews will be gathered to Israel and to Jerusalem with the deception of the Antichrist, etc, and the nations will gather against Israel. Jesus comes back and saves them, they see the scars left by the nails in His hands, and then they believe.

If you know what's happening in the newspapers and on television concerning the quest for peace in Jerusalem, you have noticed that the issue is the final status of Jerusalem. That is what this chapter tells us would happen when Jesus comes back. "The burden of the word of the Lord concerning Jerusalem..."

This chapter tells us in verse 2 that Jerusalem will be a heavy stone that causes reeling in all the people round about it, and all who lift it will hurt themselves grievously. The real issue in the Middle East will not be the final status of the Golan Heights or the West Bank or the Gaza Strip; it will be Jerusalem. Jerusalem is where Satan suffered his greatest defeat, and it is also where he will suffer his final defeat. There are tremendous spiritual forces at work in our world today, and the Middle East is increasingly going to be the centre of it.

Everything we see happening in Camp David and so on is becoming increasingly focused toward Zechariah 12. How will these events in the Middle East turn out? We know. We know what the State Department doesn't know, what the White House doesn't know, and what the United Nations doesn't know. We know that they shall look upon Him whom they have pierced, and the Jews will mourn for Him as one mourns for an only son.

That is the first corporate solidarity. Thomas is twin, Didymus, with his fellow Jews. He mirrors them. "I won't believe until I see the One who is pierced."

The second corporate solidarity that Thomas is a picture of is the scepticism of all the apostles and disciples. He's the fall guy; he gets the rap. Even in English, we have the colloquialism, 'a doubting Thomas'. That, however, is not exactly fair or accurate, although the label is stuck. This is similar to how we always talk about Peter following at a distance, saying "Oh, how could Peter follow Jesus at a distance?" — except that, apart from John, the other disciples weren't following at all. He doesn't get fair press, and neither does Thomas.

In Mark chapter 16, when we look at this synoptically, it says this (verse 11): *"And when they heard that He was alive and had been seen by her, they refused to believe it."* All the apostles were sceptical and doubting, but Thomas becomes the embodiment, the personification of their collective doubt.

Jesus revealed Himself to women first; you will always find this. But anything that God intends for good, the devil will twist to use for evil. Because of the fall of humanity, men have become insensitive and women have become hypersensitive.

Women were always more sensitive than men, but because of the fall, the difference has sharply increased. Men are reliant on female sensitivity, and women are reliant on male protection. For instance, when a husband and wife get saved, most of the time it is the wife who gets saved first. When a husband is saved and his wife is not a believer, usually — not always, but usually — the wife will become a believer; water takes the shape of its container. However, when the boots are on the other feet and a woman has an unbelieving husband, it is much more difficult. Why is it easier for women to get saved? The reason is they are more sensitive and impressionable, traits that can be either assets or liabilities. It is easier for the Lord to reveal Himself to women, because of their sensitivity. So, too, when a husband and wife pray together in seeking direction from the Lord, usually the wife will hear from the Lord first. Men are reliant on female sensitivity, because since the fall, men have become insensitive.

On the other hand, anything that God intends for good, the devil will use for evil. Because women are more sensitive, they are also more vulnerable to spiritual seduction, to being misled in hearing the voice of a counterfeit spirit and thinking it to be the voice of the Holy Spirit or to being led by their feelings. Male authority in the Bible is not based on bigger muscles; it's based on protection. The serpent beguiled the woman; Satan beguiles and seduces, and women are more vulnerable to his seduction. Thus, just as men are reliant on female sensitivity, women are reliant on male protection. That is why the leadership in a church must be male, and why the husband and father must be the spiritual head of the family.

Jesus revealed Himself to women first; the others doubted. So Thomas represents the scepticism of the other apostles.

The third corporate solidarity that Thomas represents is the one we've all encountered: he personifies human scepticism. How many times have we witnessed to somebody — a friend, a neighbour, a relative, somebody you met on the street, someone you gave a tract to — and had them say basically the same thing Thomas said: "Show me. Where is He? I can't see Him. You tell me this Jesus was crucified to take away my sin, He rose from the dead, and is now alive. You say that this crucified body is alive; well, show me. Where is He? I can't see Him. Show me this body; then I'll believe. Why should I believe your Jesus instead of Mohammad, or Buddha, or Hare Krishna? Why should I believe your book, the Bible, instead of the Bhagavad-gita, or the Book of Mormon, or the Tibetan Book of the Dead, or the Koran? What makes your book different? What makes your Jesus different? Why should I believe you? Show me! Let me see! Then I'll believe."

In trying to present the gospel to modern society, even in the American Bible belt, we're up against two things: Western rationalism, and Eastern irrationalism. Let's look first at Eastern irrationalism:

The churches in India are growing very quickly; I was in India recently. These Christians are impoverished, but their churches are growing.

Simply stated, Hinduism is not rational. When I was in India, I saw a heap of rubbish — garbage — with birds of prey pecking at the vermin crawling around in it. On top of it was a wooden frame — not a bed, but a wooden frame with some rope on it — and a baby boy, probably less than two years old, covered with lice and filth, probably HIV positive, lying on top of it and slowly dying of malnutrition. Right up the road, beautifully groomed cows are over-fed. The life of a cow is valued more highly than the life of a baby. That is their religion. "That's okay; that's his karma, because of what he did in his last life." It is not rational, but it's their religion. It's not rational for a human being to drink cow urine, but they do it. It is not rational to take water from the Ganges river and, because you believe it to be sacred, give it to an infant who dies of cholera as a result. This is not rational; you cannot tell them that the water is rife with micro-organisms and bacteria, because they believe it to be sacred. There is no reason in their religion.

It's no wonder people in India are turning from it towards Christ! As the New Testament says, our faith is rational and reasonable. It says in the book of Isaiah chapter 1 verse 18, *"Come, let us reason together, says the Lord"*. I am not saying that our faith is intellectual; it is not intellectual, but it is intellectually defensible. There is an apologetic for it — it is rational and plausible, and there is evidence for it. Hinduism is a blind faith. Yet what is very strange to me is that when I get on a plane from India and go home to England or come to the United States, I see people in the West turning from Christianity to gurus, to transcendental meditation, to New Age, to Eastern religion. Look at what those religions have done to India.

There is a church in the American south, which includes people of different racial backgrounds. The pastor has adopted children of other colour. A few generations ago in the south, that would not have been socially acceptable. At least where you had a Judeo-Christian ethic, at least where you had a biblical premise, people understood that bigotry was morally wrong and that social injustice shouldn't exist. In India, however, that's their religion. "That's his karma." Social injustice is therefore socially acceptable; it is the natural order. There is no sense of it being wrong. At least in the south there was an awareness that it was wrong and needed to be corrected, because people are all made in God's image and likeness, and Jesus died for the sin of others just as much as for ours. Not in India. Yet you see people in the West embracing these Eastern religions. I got the book "Death of a Guru", about a guru who got saved, to George Harrison of the Beatles, who is a Hindu. He builds temples for the hare krishna all over England, and he was so angered by the book that he threw it. I said, "Look, do you think that if you had been born in the slums of Calcutta instead of in the slums of Liverpool you would be living in that castle today? Look at what that religion has done to that country." A few weeks later, he was stabbed in the heart in that castle. Look at what it's done! Eastern irrationalism: it is not rational, but people believe it.

So this is what we're up against: Eastern irrationalism. The Western democracies, American society included, are post-Christian and neo- pagan. People are turning to New Age religion, even in the south. The stuff that began in California, in England and up north, is now in the south as well. I saw Vice-President Gore, who is from Arkansas, on television with Buddhist monks.

"Show me! Why should I believe your Jesus instead of Buddhism? Why should I believe your Bible instead of the Bhagavad-gita, the Tibetan Book of the Dead, or the Koran? Why should I believe your Jesus instead of Mohammad, instead of Joseph Smith? (The Mormons have a different Jesus entirely, who is not the Jesus of the Bible.) Why should I believe your Jesus instead of the one spoken of by Joseph Smith, the Jesus who is a half-brother of the devil?"

Is the answer to this because Christians are more moral? Friends, there are Protestant denominations ordaining homosexuals; Mormons won't do that. Muslims won't do that. Is it because we have such a wonderful testimony for Jesus that they'll believe us? I wish that were true. When I turn on the idiot box, I see the so-called Christian television — those con artists twisting the gospel to con money out of people, perverting the Christian message. Their god is mammon, not the true God. They are teaching the sin of covetousness and calling it 'faith'. They have faith in 'faith', not faith in Jesus. If I were not by the grace of God saved already and I turned on the television to see those con men, those heretics from hell, who are the false prophets whom Jesus warned would come in the last days — if that's what I saw, I would not want to become a Christian. I would think that being born-again was a con job. Why should the world believe us? That is what they see.

"Why should I believe? What, these con men? No. Show me, then I'll believe. I've seen the TV." I've seen the so-called Christian president from Arkansas in a so-called evangelical church in Chicago

— and noticed that his position on homosexuality and abortion-on-demand never came up. If Isaiah or Jeremiah had interviewed a king, those are the very issues they would have aimed for.

"Show me! I've heard the talk, I've seen the TV, I've seen what your born-again is, and I don't want to hear any more. Now; show me. Show me why I should believe this instead of the Mormons." There is a reason Mormonism is growing; despite the fact that what they believe is crazy, there is a reason for their growth. I have seen how Islam has grown in England. It is already beginning to grow in America. It begins in the black community — ironic, considering the fact that Islam is a religion which has never done anything but enslave black people — and right as we speak, black Christians are being murdered in the Sudan and in Nigeria by Muslims. "Show me."

We had our son's *bar mitzvah* in Israel, and while there we had a Jewish lady speak to us. She had been born in the Ukraine, in a Jewish community with 7,000 people. And of the 7,000, when the nazis invaded, three survived. Herself, her baby brother, and one other escaped miraculously. The nazis killed the rest of the Jews; all 7,000, including her parents, her brothers and her sisters. Not only did they kill them, however; they killed them in the name of Jesus Christ. My wife's parents are holocaust survivors; Jews from Romania. If you were to ask my wife's mother what the gospel of Jesus Christ is, she will tell you: the gospel of Jesus Christ is Jewish children being put into an oven in the name of the Father, the Son, and the Holy Ghost. It is difficult to explain to them the difference between a saved Christian and what they think of as Christian.

Yet this Jewish woman at my son's bar mitzvah became a believer in Jesus. How did she become a believer in Jesus when her whole family was murdered in His name? She told us the story: she met true Christians who were willing to risk their lives to save hers. When I go to Hong Kong, I go and I pick up Bibles, and pack them very carefully. I don't get my laundry done for weeks — socks, underwear, and sweaty T-shirts are the best — and I wrap the Bibles in my laundry. If a communist customs agent opens my suitcases, he will not want to search too diligently. (Before I was saved, I smuggled hashish.) When I go through to China with the Bibles, those people are hungry. They'll all take a Bible. They will listen to anything you have to say, if they know English. As a matter of fact, in some cases they'll risk their lives to take a Bible. They can be arrested for taking a Bible from a Westerner.

I know people who know a Chinese pastor who spent 34 years in prison under Mao. When the communists took over China in the late 1940's, there were no more than one million born-again believers known of in China. Going back to the time of Hudson Taylor, who began the first modern missions to China, never more than a million Christians; that's not a lot, for a country with a population the size of China's even then. Of course when the communists took over, they thought that was the end. All of the missionaries were deported back to America, Australia, and Britain, Bibles were outlawed, and all the indigenous Chinese leaders, such as Watchman Nee, were arrested. Many were killed and people thought that was the end of Christianity in China.

Until the bamboo curtain lifted just a little bit; and we found out that now the average Christian's name is not 'Smith' or 'Jones', or even 'Lieberwitz'; it is Ping. Nobody knows how many tens of millions of Christians there are in China, but they know that the churches grew under the cultural revolution.

This one Chinese pastor spent a total of 34 years in prison; the only thing he knew was prison. His whole life was prison. If you are a believer in Jesus, you go to prison. That's it. No future, no hope in this world, not even seeing your family again. He did manage to get out 34 years later, and now when he speaks, people believe him. What do those Chinese people see that makes them believe under those circumstances?

I was speaking in India in the beginning of the summer at a church that was very small. Small, but crowded. The women were sitting on the floor on mats, and the men sat around the periphery. It was jam-packed, steaming hot, in the slums of Bombay. These people were impoverished; they had nothing. Not even enough Bibles. They are ex-Hindus, ex-Sikhs. The persecution against Christians in India by militant Hindus is increasing; they have burned some. Yet this church was packed out. These people were hungry, desperate for the Word of God.

What was making those Hindus believe?

I go to Africa a lot. When I was in Africa last spring (which is their autumn), I got some reports from missionaries in the Sudan. The

Muslims were burning little children from the ages of five to nine; they began with the five-year-olds and burned their brothers and sisters in age order, younger to older, in an attempt to get them to deny Jesus Christ. These little black children refused to deny Jesus. These are children, ages five to nine. The growth of militant Islam in Africa is astounding; but so is the growth of the gospel. We hear about churches being burned in Nigeria all the time. (I wouldn't expect the president to speak up for the rights of Christians in Nigeria, either, by the way.)

What is it that makes those African people believe, when they're going to be burned? When they're going to see children burned? Why do they believe?

I know the story of another Jewish Christian, whose name is Richard Wurmbrand. He's a Romanian Jew; my wife's family knew him even before he was saved. He was in prison for 14 years with his wife under the communist dictator Nikolai Ceaescu. He wrote the book, "Tortured for Christ", and told a story about the torture cell, or the interrogation cell, where he was taken. It was a small room; there were 30 to 40 prisoners who would be systematically beaten and tortured daily, until they either talked or died. Sometimes Richard Wurmbrand would wake up in the morning to find that the people on either side of him were dead, usually from internal hemorrhage. He did not know if he would be alive the next day himself.

But he told the story of two people whom he saw in that interrogation cell: one was a Romanian scientist, who was arrested by the communist police because he had not been a member of the party; that was his crime. He was a member of the National Academy of Science in Bucharest, arrested because the communists were paranoid of any intellectual whom they did not control. This scientist was an atheist; he did not believe in God.

But then there was a Romanian peasant who had become a saved Christian, apparently through a Plymouth Brethren church. This peasant would try to witness and share the gospel with the other people in the interrogation cell, and the scientist would mock him every day. The scientist would say to him, "Look at you. Your God is so powerful; you want me to believe in your God? If your God is so powerful, why doesn't your God get you out of here? Your God loves you? If I loved someone who was in here, and I had the power to get them out, I wouldn't leave them here. Yet you want me to believe in your God? Why should I believe in your God? Why doesn't He get you out of here?"

The peasant replied, "My God doesn't take me out of here because He loves you, too, and He wants me to tell you about Him before it's too late, because you're going to meet Him soon."

The peasant told him that, and the scientist mocked him more. "Look at you! They're doing to you what they do to us, yet you tell me about your Jesus and I see you singing these hymns to yourself, muttering like an old fool. When you talk to your Jesus, does He talk back to you?"

The peasant said, "Yes, He talks back to me."

"What does He tell you when He talks back to you?" the scientist demanded.

"He tells me He loves me, and is coming to take me home soon," the peasant replied.

The scientist continued sardonically: "And what happens when He talks to you? Does He smile at you?"

"Oh, yes, He smiles," the peasant answered.

"Well, what does He look like when He smiles?" the scientist sneered.

The peasant said, "Like this." And Richard Wurmbrand reports that he does not know what he saw, but somehow that scientist saw the Shekinah glory of God. He fell down on the floor and began pounding his fists, crying and saying, "You've seen Jesus Christ! You've seen Jesus Christ!"

What made that atheist scientist believe? What did he see?

But then there's the Book. Our Book. "Come, let us reason together." In Luke's gospel, we see what happened when Jesus rose from the dead and met the disciples on the road to Emmaus. In verse 27 of chapter 24, *"Beginning with Moses and the prophets, He explained to them the things concerning Himself from all the scriptures."* The Bible is examinable. The way I got saved was by trying to disprove the Bible when I was in university. I first tried to disprove it with science, then with history and archaeology. Yet the more I tried to disprove the Bible, the more evidence I found for believing in it. It got to the point that it took me more faith to reject Jesus Christ than it did to accept Him.

Imagine someone saying that 800 years from now somebody was going to be born, naming his ancestors, detailing that he would die by crucifixion — this written six centuries before crucifixion was invented; that was a Roman method of execution, not a Jewish one — that he would be betrayed by his friend, the price this friend would betray him for, that they would gamble for his clothes and give him gall to drink when he was hanging on the cross, and that he would make the Gentile nations believe in the Jewish God. Jews account for less than one percent of the world's population; much less. Why do people in Tennessee and Tonga and Toronto, in Taiwan and Tanzania believe in the Jewish God? Isaiah 11 says that the nations will be brought to the Root of Jesse. Dozens and dozens of prophesies which the prophets had no control over, nor could anyone purposely fulfil them about himself. And just as every prophecy about His first coming was actually, literally fulfilled, so all the prophecies about His return are being fulfilled as we go about our daily lives. From the events in the Middle East to the backslidden state of the Western church, every prediction about the return of Jesus is taking place.

"Come, let us reason"; Jesus explained the gospel from the scriptures. Nobody who picked up the Bible would, through reading it, become a Mormon. Nobody who simply picked up the Bible, or even just the New Testament, would ever become a Jehovah's Witness by that means. Nobody would ever pick up the Bible and wind up a Roman Catholic. But there are thousands upon thousands of people who were never witnessed to, who got saved simply by reading the New Testament. I know people who were saved just by reading the gospel of John. Nobody ever became a Mormon, a Jehovah's Witness, or a Catholic by reading the New Testament. But countless people have been born again through reading it. Our faith is plausible.

People are not going to come to believe in Jesus by seeing a show. On the contrary, don't get me wrong; I am moderately Pentecostal myself, but Jesus said directly, *"A wicked and an adulterous generation seeks after a sign."* When you see people flocking to stadiums and auditoriums and arenas to see the kind of maniacal behaviour displayed by those who follow the Toronto experience, that is wickedness and adultery. "These signs follow"; Jesus never allowed a show to be the focus of His message or His ministry. He had healings — only His healings were real and could be medically authenticated, unlike the bogus things you often see today — but He never had a healing crusade. He had a repentance crusade. He had miracles, but never a miracle crusade. He had a repentance crusade. He never allowed signs and wonders to be the focus of His ministry; that's what the Antichrist and the False Prophet are going to do. Now, I believe in signs and wonders understood biblically, but not what you see today. That's not going to cause people to believe. I've seen witch doctors in Africa put on shows that would make your hair stand on end; I've seen things done in the jungles of Indonesia that you would not believe people could do. It's demonic power. But you know what? There are so-called 'saved Christians' in Pensacola, Florida, who are taking part in the same kinds of manifestations and calling it the Holy Ghost. New Age is rife in the church. So why should the world believe us?

"Show me! Let me see! I've seen all the hype, I've heard all the jargon, I've grown up in Tennessee or Kentucky or Arkansas, I've heard the gospel my whole life in Sunday school. But I'm still not saved; why should I believe? Show me. I've heard enough, I've heard; I've heard, now I want to see. Show me! Show me this Jesus! Show me this crucified body, which you say is alive. Then I'll believe."

"Now you are Christ's body; individually members of it" (I Corinthians 12:27).

What do those people see in China that makes them want to believe? What makes them so hungry for a Bible that they'll take it, even though they know if they get caught with it they'll get sent to prison? What makes them want it so much? What do they see in China that people don't see in America?

Those Africans — little children being murdered by Muslims as we congregate freely! Those churches in Africa are growing like wildfire. Oh, they have a lot of problems; a shortage of leadership and a shortage of good Bible teaching, but whatever their problems are, evangelism and seeing people get saved isn't one of them. Why are those churches exploding in Ghana and in Kenya despite persecution? What do they see? What do those Africans see that people don't see in Britain?

What did those Jews see in Eastern Europe that made them believe? When your whole family is murdered in the name of Jesus Christ, what could make you believe that He is your Messiah? What did she see?

What did that Romanian scientist see in that communist prison that made him believe? What makes somebody like that believe?

In India, despite the unbelievable poverty, opposition from the Hindus, what is making those people believe? What is making those people turn from Eastern religion at a time when people in the West are turning to it? What do they see?

What do those Indians see? What do those Chinese see? What do those Jews see? What do those Africans see? What did that communist cell have to offer that atheist scientist? What do they see?

They see a crucified Body that's been resurrected, a church that loves not its life even unto death. That's what they see.

Why is America post-Christian, neo-pagan? The plight of America is not primarily the fault of the abortionists. The plight of America is not primarily the fault of crooked businessmen on Wall Street and crooked politicians in Washington. It is not primarily the fault of militant homosexuals and lesbians or pornographers in Hollywood. The plight of America is primarily the fault of a compromised, back-slidden, lukewarm church. We think America is America. When God looks down from heaven, however, He doesn't see Memphis or New York or Los Angeles; He sees Laodicea.

"Show me! Show me, and then I'll believe! I've heard, I've heard, I've heard; now I want to see. I've been hearing my whole life. Southern Baptists are members of the Ku Klux Klan; I've heard. The money preachers on TV; I've heard! I don't want to hear any more; now I want to see. Now I want to see. Show me that crucified body that's been resurrected; then I will believe your Jesus Christ. Show me what makes your book better than the Book of Mormon or the Koran or the Tibetan Book of the Dead; then I'll believe. Where is this crucified body?"

When Africans ask where the crucified body is, the African Christians can say something we cannot say: "You're looking at it."

Those people under the communists in Eastern Europe, when they wanted to see a crucified body, they didn't have to look too far. Those Christians in China, those Christians in India, when they are asked, "Where is the crucified body?" They can say, "Here it is." In America, in the Bible belt, where is the crucified body?

Some con man on television, calling himself a Christian and perverting the scriptures, is something we can show them. People falling on the floor in drunken hysterics, imitating animals, we can show them that. A so-called Christian president in a so-called Christian church dodging the issues of abortion and homosexuality — we can show them that. But can we show them a crucified body, living and breathing and walking in the power of the resurrection? Not in America. Not even in the Bible belt. If you want to see that, you have to go to China. If you want to see that, you have to go to Africa. If you want to see that, you have to go to India.

They don't believe any more. Given what's become of us, what the state of the Western church is, what the world sees on the idiot box — frankly, while I don't justify their unbelief, I cannot blame them for it either. They don't believe us any more, and I wish I could say I blamed them. But they don't believe us because we are not believable.

When will they believe again? I don't say that we have to be persecuted. But we do have to be willing to be persecuted if that's what it takes. Let us not deceive ourselves; persecution will come to the believing church in America. The only reason we've had this freedom is the influence of the Bible on our models of culture, government, etc. Now that we've turned from that, persecution is not far away.

Persecution comes from the devil; it is bad. "Satan will put some of you in prison", Jesus told the church in Sardis, but God has a purpose in it. If you want to see a real church, look at a persecuted one. Only people who really love Jesus will be willing to die for Him. Those Christians in India couldn't dream of having the kinds of buildings our churches have. They couldn't dream of supporting a full-time pastor. They couldn't imagine it! But they are the rich ones. We are bankrupt. They've got the real riches. They have the real jewels. We have the buildings.

"Show me. Show me!"

When will America believe again? When will the "Bible belt" mean anything again? When will the American people begin really believing? It's only going to happen one way: when they say, "Show me", and we can say, "Here it is."

I am sorry to say this; I love America, I was born there, and I care about that country. But I've seen too much of the world, and I've seen too much of what the Word of God said would happen in the Last Days, not to say these terrible things.

This is it. These are the Last Days. If you had asked me fifteen

155

years ago why I believed it was the Last Days, I would have pointed to events in the Middle East — and I still believe that. I would have pointed to the globalisation of the world economy and the destruction of the environment — and I still believe that. But the clearest sign now of the soon return of Jesus is the deception within what is supposedly the believing church. Jesus warned about deception perpetrated against the elect four times more than He did famines, earthquakes, wars, rumours of wars, the Middle East — He warned about that more than anything else; yet we are so deceived. We don't even know where we are. We think we're in America; we don't know we're in Laodicea.

When will they believe again? They've heard, they've heard, they've heard; most people growing up in Tennessee have heard the gospel their whole lives. There are people in the Bible belt who have heard the gospel every Sunday night for thirty years, but they don't believe.

"Faith cometh by hearing, and hearing by the Word of God", yes. Faith also comes by seeing a crucified body. When will they believe? They will believe when we can say what the Africans, the Chinese, the Jews, and the Indians can say. Where is the crucified life? When you can say, "here it is", then and only then will people believe, because then and only then will they see something worth believing in.

Egypt, Babylon and the Palm of God

We have spoken a number of times concerning things that teach about the last days. There are a number of time-periods in Israel's history, outlined in the Bible that prefigure what will happen in the last days.

In watching news reports about the riots on the Temple Mount recently, I was reminded of one of the things that convinces me that we are in the last days. Specifically, there is much arguing over the propriety of custody of the Temple Mount.

I learned yesterday that a major American university in Massachusetts has banned their evangelical students' fellowship. It has been banned from the campus as a hate group, because of their belief that homosexuality is wrong. Although this is under appeal, it sets a national precedent. If you believe what the Bible says about unnatural sex, the Bible becomes hate literature and you become a hate group, and the First Amendment does not protect inciting hatred. This also convinces me that it is the last days.

When I look at the apostasy in the church — the people on their way to ecumenical unity, Pensacola and other similar demonic deceptions — all of these things point to the last days.

I, of course, live in England, and I see what's happening: how people are having a single currency shoved down their throats even when they don't want it, how they're going into a federal, nondemocratic Europe — entailing not just the loss of national sovereignty but also the loss of democracy — the decisions made by bureaucrats behind closed doors whom you did not vote for and cannot believe in. These things are being forced on people, yet they are sitting back and taking it. Of course, parliamentary democracy in its modern sense was born out of the influences of biblical Christianity, and now that Christianity has been abandoned in Europe, all the democracies that Christianity helped give rise to will likewise be abandoned.

Persecution of the church is already looming in America; if you don't agree with homosexuality , you are a bigot, and it becomes the equivalent of a hate crime to speak against such things.

The last days of the first century, before the temple was destroyed in 70 AD, is one of the things that teaches about the end. The last days of Samaria in 720 BC is another thing that teaches about the end. However, we are now looking at about 585 BC, the last days of Judah before the Babylonian captivity. Above all else in the Old Testament, this teaches about the end. It is evident in the New Testament where it talks about eschatology — especially in the teaching of Jesus about the last days — that the themes from the books of Isaiah, Jeremiah, and Ezekiel about the Babylonian captivity are being recycled. The destruction of the temple talked about by Jesus in Matthew 24 and Luke 21 comes straight out of Jeremiah. Jesus warns repeatedly about false prophets, and this theme is also prominent in the major prophets. "Fallen, fallen is Babylon" in the book of Revelation comes straight out of Isaiah and Jeremiah.

The same things that happened in the last days of Judah, when Jeremiah's message was rejected, will happen in the last days full stop, both to the Jews and to the church. It will be repeated; remember that a Judeo-Christian perspective of prophecy regards it as cyclical.

Let us begin to understand this: what will happen to faithful churches and the faithful remnant in the last days? What should we expect? There are various teachings that could explain some of this; for example, the Maccabees. However, we're looking at it now from the point of view of the Babylonian captivity.

In Jeremiah chapter 40, the captivity is underway. Nebuchadnezzar invades Jerusalem four times. What you see happening right now, with the interfaith movement, the ecumenical movement, and the New Age movement, is about the Babylonian captivity. During the Middle Ages, Martin Luther came to realise there had been a Babylonian captivity of the church under the medieval papacy. He understood the spiritual character of Babylon; this marriage of the political system of the world to a corrupt religious system. This was the 'Holy Roman Empire', which was neither holy nor Roman. This will happen again. We can see the captivity coming. There are people everywhere who believe in having one 'apostle' over a city, which is an ancient error begun by Ignatius of Antioch that is called mono-episcopacy. That is how the papacy began to evolve; it is an ancient deception that is making its comeback. The problem, of course, is that most of my fellow Pentecostals and Charismatics are too ignorant to realise that these are things that have happened in the past, which will result in the same thing that happened in the past — a Babylonian captivity of the church.

Let us begin in chapter 40 of Jeremiah:

"Then the word of the LORD came to Jeremiah from the LORD, after Nebuzaradan, captain of the bodyguard, had released him from Ramah, when he had taken him bound in chains from among the exiles of Jerusalem and Judah who were exiled to Babylon. Now the captain of the guard had taken Jeremiah and said to him, 'The LORD your God promised this calamity against this place, and the LORD has brought it on it and done just as He promised, because you people sinned against the LORD and did not listen to His voice. Therefore this thing has happened to you. But now, behold, I am freeing you today from the chains which are on your hands. If you would prefer to come with me to Babylon, come along, and I will look after you. But if you would prefer not to come to Babylon, never mind – look, the whole land is before you. Go wherever it seems good and right for you to go.' As Jeremiah was still not going back, he said, 'Go on back, then, to Gedaliah the son of Ahikam the son of Shaphan, whom the king of Babylon has appointed over the cities of Judah, and stay with him among the people. Or else go anywhere it seems right for you to go.' And the captain of the guard gave him a ration and let him go.

Then Jeremiah went to Mizpah, to Gedaliah the son of Ahikam, and stayed with him among the people who were left in the land. Now all the commanders of the forces that were in the field, they and their men, heard that the king of Babylon had appointed Gedaliah the son of Ahikam over the land, and that he had put him in charge of the men, women and children, those of the poorest of the land who had not been exiled to Babylon.

So they came to Gedaliah at Mizpah, along with Ishmael the son of Nethaniah, and Johanan and Jonathan the sons of Kareah, and Seraiah the son of Tanhumeth, the sons of Ephai the Netophathite, and Jezaniah the son of a Maachathite, both they and their men.

Then Gedaliah the son of Ahikam the son of Shaphan swore to them and their men, saying, 'Do not be afraid of serving the Chaldeans. Stay in the land and serve the king of Babylon, that it may go well with you.'" (Now, the king of Babylon is a metaphor for the devil, and a type of the antichrist. We see this in Isaiah chapter 14.)

'Now as for me, behold, I am going to stay at Mizpah to stand for you before the Chaldeans who come to us. But as for you, gather in wine and summer fruit and oil, and put them in your storage vessels, and live in your cities that you have taken over .'

Likewise also, all the Jews who are in Moab and among the sons of Amon and in Edom, who were in the other countries, heard that the king of Babylon had left a remnant for Judah, and that he had appointed over them Gedaliah the son of Ahikam the son of Shaphan. And all the Jews returned from all the places to which they had been driven away, and came to the land of Judah, to Gedaliah at Mizpah, and gathered their wine and summer fruit in great abundance.

Now, Johanan the son of Kareah and all the commanders of the forces that were in the field came to Gedaliah at Mizpah, and said to him, 'Are you well aware that Baalis the king of the sons of Amon has sent Ishmael the son of Nethaniah to take your life?' But Gedaliah the son of Ahikam did not believe them.

Then Johanan the son of Kareah spoke secretly to Gedaliah at Mizpah, saying, 'Let me go and kill Ishmael the son of Nethaniah, and not a man will know. Why should he take your life so that all of the Jews who are gathered to you would be scattered, and the remnant of Judah perish?'

But Gedaliah the son of Ahikam said to Johanan the son of Kareah, 'Do not do this thing, for you are telling a lie about Ishmael'.

Now it came about in the seventh month that Ishmael the son of

Nethaniah the son of Elishama of the royal family and one of the chief officials of the king, along with ten men, came to Mizpah to Gedaliah the son of Ahikam. While they were eating bread together they were in Mizpah. Ishmael the son of Nethaniah and the ten men who were with him arose and struck down Gedaliah the son of Ahikam the son of Shaphan with the sword, and put to death the one the king of Babylon had appointed over the land.

Ishmael also struck down all of the Jews that were with him, that is, with Gedaliah at Mizpah, and the Chaldeans who were found there, the men of war. Now it happened on the next day of the killing of Gedaliah, when no one knew about it, that eighty men came from Shechem of Shiloh where the ark had formerly been, and from Samaria with their beards shaved, their clothes torn, and their bodies gashed, having grain offerings and incense in their hands to bring to the house of the LORD.

Then Ishmael the son of Nethaniah went out from Mizpah to meet them, weeping as he went. And it came about as he came that he said to them, 'Come to Gedaliah the son of Ahikam!'

Yet it happened that as soon as they entered the city, Ishmael the son of Nethaniah and the men that were with him slaughtered them and cast them into the cistern."

The faithful remnant of the last days of Judah faced what the faithful remnant of the last days of the church will face. They had three choices: Egypt, a figure of the world; Babylon, a figure of false religion; or the palm of God. Now notice that it was the word of the LORD that came to Jeremiah; the Hebrew word for 'word' is *dvar*, which is the Hebrew equivalent of the Greek word *logos*. As we speak about on the 'When They Burn the Scroll' tape, this is not about "having a word, having a word, having a word". It is an encounter with Christ in the Old Testament. The same Jesus active in the New Testament is in the Old Testament, and the same Holy Spirit that communicates Him to us in the New Testament communicated Jesus in an Old Testament sense to the prophets of Israel. The Word; it was a Christological encounter. Once more, as we talk about on the Jeremiah 36 tapes, false prophets will always give you "*a* word". True prophets will point you to "*the* Word".

To continue, everyone knew now that Jeremiah was right; all the false prophets with the big talk and the big mouths were gone.

Nothing they had said came to pass; they were proven wrong. However, in spite of the proof that they were wrong, people still continued to believe them.

"The prophets prophesy falsely and My people love it so."

This applies today; we have men such as Michael Brown, Rick Joyner, Benny Hinn, etc. — you know who they are — who prophesy falsely. Yet people will follow these men in an act of direct rebellion, and a time will come when they will reap the consequences of that; the captivity will take place. It is a remnant — and only a remnant — who do not go into captivity. The remnant, we see in verse seven, was in fact comprised of the poorest of the land.

Do not expect the high and mighty — the mega-churches — do not expect the Christians who are caught up in affluence, who are caught up in doctrines designed to produce material benefit, do not expect the big figures you see on what is erroneously referred to as "Christian" television, to survive; they will not survive. They will go to Babylon. It will be the poorest of the land who survive. However, when this happens, God is taking care of His people, though the king of Babylon never loses sight of his designs. He wants to dominate and rule everything.

This was a time of tremendous famine; there were severe food shortages. The Babylonians imitated the Assyrians in that they made war by siege. They would starve people into submission. The idea of food shortage, or famine, in both the Old and New Testaments, is what the prophet Amos describes as a 'famine for the hearing of the Word of God'. The physical famine becomes a metaphor for a spiritual famine. But for the faithful remnant, we see in verse 12, there will be great abundance.

The kinds of sermons heard in small, faithful churches every Sunday, the kinds of Bible studies conducted by faithful Christians, are increasingly rare. There are people who would come to these churches or studies from other churches or studies never having heard anything like their teaching before. There are people who have been in the Charismatic movement for 30 years who have never been to a Bible study. It may seem ludicrous to us, but it is true. A few verses out of context and a lot of hype and pop psychology is the extent of the Bible teaching they have had. They have never even heard exposition of scripture. In their extrabiblical reading you will find nothing but more pop psychology and hype artistry; they have never read any good teaching, such as A. W. Tozer's work.

The faithful, however, though they may be a minority and they may be the poorest of the land, will have an abundance of food. These faithful, in terms of spiritual things, have a lot to eat. They know things about the antichrist, the last days, and other concepts of which most Christians have no idea. The majority is being set up for the Babylonian captivity and they don't even know it. But the few, the poor, the small, the faithful — they will survive. Knowledge is power; the majority has no food. They have no people who are capable of teaching them.

Yet for the sake of trying to keep peace, Gedaliah tries to tell people to honour the king of Babylon. "Look, we have to go along with the system; we don't want to be deported too. We don't want to find ourselves re- scattered. We don't want to be taken away; we want to keep what we have, so we have to agree to pay homage; go along with the system." This is very much what happened in the first century. The reason the early Christians got themselves into trouble was not what they believed, but their refusal to pay homage to the emperor, who at that time had become the equivalent of the king of Babylon. The mystery religions of pagan Babylon were now in Rome, in the pantheon, and the emperor as the pontiff was the head of it. What the king of Babylon was in Jeremiah's day, the emperor was in the first century. It was not what they believed, but what they did not believe that got them into trouble. "You can believe what you want, as long as you go along with the program." We will find this mindset increasing in the last days, even among the faithful remnant. We will have visible leaders who will try to compromise with Babylon, and they will give you what seem to be pastoral reasons: "I'm trying to protect you." "I'm trying to secure what we have, to preserve what remains." Even among the faithful remnant, expect a concerted effort to bring you into line with the status quo. They will come with very persuasive and very logical arguments along that line.

God will judge such people and their motives; they won't survive either. Gedaliah was even warned to stop what he was doing, that he was going to get himself killed; but he refused to listen. Do not think for one moment that you can make some kind of peace with the king of Babylon. Do not think that there can be any accommodation or cessation of hostilities. We cannot 'get along' with the king of Babylon.

They were invited to come to Babylon; that was their first choice. Is your church going to join the ecumenical movement? Is your denomination going to join the World Council of Churches? The false prophet will eventually gain control over this and use it to support the antichrist. That's the first choice; expect it to happen in the last days. You will find people who will try to rationalise and gloss over the issues – 'Well, maybe I don't agree with them, and I understand that we're the faithful remnant, but we have to try to get along with them.' We will find this being said; but ultimately, there is nothing in that but death. Notice that not only did Gedaliah die, but those of the poor and simple who followed him died with him. Down that road lies death; there is no peace with Babylon.

More than that, Babylon cannot be changed. Let's look at Jeremiah 51. Babylon is under judgment in verse 49; Babylon is to fall for the slain of Israel. In verse 60 Jeremiah writes on a scroll of the calamities that will come on Babylon. In verse 24, it says that God will repay Babylon for what Babylon has done. But in verse 6 Jeremiah is saying, *'Flee from the midst of Babylon; each of you save his life.'* In other words, 'Get out of there!' Get out of ecumenical denominations; God's purpose is to destroy them.

In verse 9, we find that there was attempted healing applied to Babylon, but she was not healed. *Babylon cannot be healed.* It has not changed from the time of the Tower of Babel to the Babylonian empire to what you see in the book of Revelation; it cannot change. One of today's myths is this: the Roman Catholic Church has changed since the second Vatican Council. Well, the second Vatican Council documents all affirm the Council of Trent. You have two kinds of doctrine in the Roman Catholic church: *proxima fadi* and *di fadi*. A *proxima fadi* doctrine can be changed; the pagan mass can be changed from Latin to English. A *di fadi* doctrine cannot be changed; the mass itself cannot be changed, nor can purgatory or any doctrine like it. The Roman Catholic church admits this.

Jeremiah 51:19 says that all of mankind is stupid, devoid of knowledge. People are stupid; Jeremiah uses very strong terms. Throughout his book, he says things that would sound crude if we were to say them. He uses two different words for human stupidity, and neither one of them is pleasant. Look at Jeremiah chapter 10:8 –

"But they are altogether stupid and foolish in their discipline of delusion." One of the words he uses for 'stupid' means a perversion of logic to justify what is known to be wrong. People know that certain things are wrong, but they pervert their logic in order to ease their conscience. When Jeremiah says they are stupid, he doesn't mean they are congenitally stupid, that they are slow learners or have a birth defect. He means that they willfully pervert their logic. This is exactly what we see happening today; people who should know better, even theologians like J. I. Packer, are perverting their logic. And what is the purpose of it? To make a deal with Babylon. But those who follow Gedaliah will wind up like Gedaliah.

The first offer to be made then, is an invitation to go to Babylon. But let us continue. Jeremiah 41:16 –

> "Then Johanan the son of Kareah and all the commanders of the forces that were with him took from Mizpah all the remnant of the people who had recovered from Ishmael the son of Nethaniah after he had struck down Gedaliah the son of Ahikam; that is, the men who were soldiers, the women, the children, and the eunuchs whom he had brought back to Gibeon"

Johanan did not hate Gedaliah; he simply tried to warn him to stop being so naïve, or he would go to destruction and bring the people with him. Expect the Johanans who say that to be ignored, just as they ignore the Jeremiahs until it is too late. Just as they found out that Jeremiah was right, so they also found out that Johanan was right. Ultimately, however, what is left is that which is pure. There is a sifting process in motion here; the deception comes, but even the deception that comes from Babylon is part of the sifting process. The Lord only wants those who are really, really right.

Let us look at what happens: Johanan gathers them, and in verse 17 he brings them back from Gibeon.

> "And they went and stayed in Geruth Kimham, which is next to Bethlehem, in order to proceed into Egypt because of the Chaldeans, for they were afraid of them since Ishmael the son of Nethaniah had struck down Gedaliah the son of Ahikam, whom the king of Babylon had appointed over the land."

They go to Geruth Kimham, which is next to Bethlehem. We must understand why they did that: By this time, the throne of David had been lost. There was no longer a living descendant of David on the throne. Their longing was for the house of David to be restored, which they began to see in Messianic terms. The whole concept of the Messiah, while it was always there, really begins to develop and evolve after the captivity. They *knew* about the Messiah, but it really began to crystallise and clarify after the captivity; that He would restore this lineage of David. God had promised the Jews that there would always be a descendant of David on the throne of David; now either Jesus is spiritually on the throne of David, and will one day rule from Jerusalem on the throne of David, or God has broken His promise, which scripture tells us He cannot do.

Geruth Kimham means "the lodge of pining". It was situated next to Bethlehem, which was the city of David, where the house of David had originated. So they are pining the loss of the lineage of David, and longing for it to be restored. That is why they go to Geruth Kimham. What you will find in the last days among the remnant is this: they will go to Geruth Kimham. They will reach such a state of despair that their only aspiration is the return of Jesus. They realise that nothing will ever make it the way it used to be; nothing will restore Christianity to what it had historically been. Nothing except the return of Christ. The church becomes a lodge of pining, where the only hope we have to hold onto is the promise of Jesus' coming. We will see this desperation.

However, in the midst of that desperation, the pressures of practical reality begin to set in. So, not wanting to go to Babylon – that didn't work, and the ones who tried it are dead – the next temptation is to go to Egypt, which, as we know from Jeremiah 30:31 and many other places in scripture, is really going to the world for help. In the beginning, Egypt is Egypt and Babylon is Babylon. Nobody at this point expected that Babylon would also conquer Egypt. Ultimately, the antichrist gets practically all of it. There were some Jews who found refuge in Edom, and it's interesting to see in Daniel that that area seems to escape some of what the antichrist will be able to do. The area of Petra, it would appear from Daniel, provides some refuge. For some reason, it will not be under antichrist's domain to the same degree. This is very mysterious, and I don't fully understand it. However, there were Jews going there; that is where some of the faithful remnant went when Jerusalem was under siege. It would appear from Isaiah chapter 16 and others that there is some future eschatological significance to this area around Petra in Edom. We take our Bible study tours to Petra sometimes; every few years we go to Jordan.

Nonetheless, that is a separate subject. Let's look more closely at Geruth Kimham. Under this pressure, there comes a pressure to go to the world for help. The same thing happens with Hezekiah in Isaiah 30 and 31; it becomes an issue again. They fear the Babylonians, so they go to the world. The world, its governments, its legal systems, etc. – it will not protect us in the last days. The only reason that any government has at any time protected the rights of Christians is because of Christian influence in that government. Paul instructed the churches to pray for those in authority, even the pagan emperor, that they might lead peaceable lives. Paul himself appealed to Caesar; we can do that, but ultimately Caesar too, who is another figure of antichrist, turned against the early church. The world offers nothing, but things become so desperate that many people will want to go to the world.

Let's continue in chapter 42 verse 1:

"Then all the commanders of the forces, Johanan son of Kareah, Jezaniah son of Hoshaiah, and all the people, both small and great, approached and said to Jeremiah the prophet, 'Please let our petition come before you, and pray for us to the LORD your God – that is for all this remnant, because we are left but a few out of many, as your own eyes now see us – that the LORD your God would tell us the way in which we should walk and the thing that we should do.'

Then Jeremiah the prophet said to them, 'I have heard you. Behold, I am going to pray to the LORD your God in accordance with your words. And it will come about that the whole message which the LORD will answer you, I will tell you. I will not keep back a word from you.'

Then they said to Jeremiah, 'May the LORD be a true and faithful Witness against us if we do not act in accordance with the whole message which the LORD your God will send you to us. Whether it is pleasant or unpleasant, we will listen to the voice of the LORD our God, to Whom we are sending you, that it may go well with us when we listen to the voice of the LORD our God.'"

The faithful remnant knows that Jeremiah is a true prophet, and that all the other guys to whom the kings were listening were liars and deceivers who are now either dead or in Babylon. The faithful church will ask, "What should we do, Lord? We're in this situation in Geruth Kimham, we're longing for Jesus to come back, for His kingdom – it's the only hope we have. But on one hand, we can't go to Babylon – look what happened to those who tried it – and on the other hand, the only alternative seems to be Egypt. What should we do? We'll listen to You; we'll do whatever the LORD says." Well, unfortunately, during times of pressure there are Christians who will say, "We will do whatever the LORD says, as long as it's in agreement with what we want."

Jeremiah 42:7 –

> "Now it came about at the end of ten days that the word of the LORD came to Jeremiah."

Notice that; Jeremiah went and sought the Lord, and the Lord answered ten days later. Be careful of people who think they can go around prophesying and giving words and hearing from the Lord this, this, this and that; that is clairvoyance and soothsaying, not prophecy. True prophets don't go around claiming that kind of revelation all the time. What they do is point people to the scripture, and if they do get a revelation, it's always based on scripture. Jeremiah seeks God. Now, ten days is a significant figure in the Bible. Forty and ten are the two numbers most associated in scripture with testing. If you recall, in Revelation 2:10 Jesus says that the church of Smyrna will be persecuted and put in prison for ten days, and this seems to correspond to the ten major periods of persecution under the emperors.

Jeremiah 42:8 –

> "Then he called for Johanan the son of Kareah and all the commanders of the forces that were with him, and for all the people, both small and great, and said, 'Thus says the LORD God of Israel, to whom you sent me to present your petition before Him: "If you will indeed stay in this land, then I will build you up and not tear you down; I will plant you and not uproot you, for I will relent concerning the calamity I have inflicted on you. Do not be afraid of the king of Babylon, whom you are now fearing. Do not be afraid of him,' declares the LORD, 'for I am with you to save you and deliver you from his hand. I

will also show you compassion, so that he will have compassion on you and restore you to your own soil.

"But if you are going to say, 'We will not stay in this land,' so as not to listen to the voice of the LORD your God, saying, 'No, but we will go to the land of Egypt, where we shall not see war or hear the sound of a trumpet or hunger for bread, and we will stay there,' in that case, listen to the word of the LORD, O remnant of Judah: Thus says the LORD God of hosts, the God of Israel: if you really set your mind to go into Egypt and reside there, it will come about that the sword which you are afraid of will overtake you there in the land of Egypt, and the famine about which you are anxious will follow closely after you there in Egypt, and you will die there.

So all the men who set their minds to go to Egypt and reside there will die of the sword, of famine, and of pestilence, and they will have no survivors or refugees from the calamity that I am going to bring on them. For thus says the LORD of hosts, the God of Israel, as My anger and wrath have been poured out on the inhabitants of Jerusalem, so My anger and wrath will be poured out on you when you enter Egypt, and you will become a curse, an object of horror, an imprecation and a reproach, and you will see this place no more.'

The LORD has spoken to you, O remnant of Judah: Do not go into Egypt. You should clearly understand that this day I have testified against you, for you have only deceived yourselves. For it is you who sent me to the LORD your God, saying, 'Pray for us to the LORD our God, and whatever the LORD our God says, tell us so we will do it.' So I have told you today, but you have not obeyed the LORD your God, even in whatever He has sent me to tell you. Therefore you should now clearly understand that you will die by the sword, by famine and by pestilence in the place where you wish to go to reside."

Well, they went to Egypt; they went to the world. Let's understand this: they did not go to the world because they were seeking the carnal pleasures of Egypt. They went to the world in a time of great duress – fear of the king of Babylon. When the Antichrist comes, he is going to invoke a tremendous fear. Those dwelling at Geruth Kimham will have that choice: Do we go into Babylon? Do we go into Egypt? Do we go into the interfaith movement, or do we simply go to the world? Or do we place ourselves in the hand of God, remain where we are, and trust Him?

That was the choice they had, and that will be the choice faced by the faithful remnant in the last days: Egypt, Babylon, or the palm of God. Those who went to Babylon found death. Those who went to Egypt were pursued by the sword and by famine in the world. *There is no safety in Egypt.* But God says, *"Don't be afraid of the king of Babylon. If you will stay in this land I will build you up and not tear you down. I will plant you and not uproot you."* God's promise is always good, though it is very difficult to see and believe that when all around you is calamity: the sword, the famine, the king of Babylon whose power seems invincible. Yet that will be the choice, and there were and will again be people, even in the good churches, who make the wrong choice. However, once more, they will have been warned.

Let's go a bit further: in chapter 43:1-3 it says this:

> "But it came about that as soon as Jeremiah, whom the LORD their God had sent, had finished telling all the people the words of the LORD their God — that is, all the words — that Azariah the son of Hoshaiah and Johanan the son of Kareah and all the arrogant men said to Jeremiah, 'You are telling a lie. The LORD our God has not sent you to say, 'You are not to enter Egypt to reside there'. But Baruch the son of Neriah is inciting you against us to give us over into the hand of the Chaldeans so they may put us to death or exile in Babylon.'"

First the backslidden nation and its leaders and false prophets rejected Jeremiah. But the heat gets so intense in the last days of Judah that even in the faithful remnant there is a rejection of Jeremiah, orchestrated by the arrogant among them. It would almost seem to be a contradiction in terms; how could there be people in the faithful remnant who are arrogant? You know what? If you want to see a big mess today, look at discernment ministries. The very ones who realise the nature of deception, the ones who realise what Pensacola and Toronto are, and what the ecumenical movement is, the very ones who know that these things are wrong – the very ones who understand the demonic nature of faith- prosperity preaching, the ones who understand what's wrong – within the ranks of those organisations you will find good and bad; and yes, you will find people who are downright arrogant.

Jewel van der Merwe is under tremendous attack at the moment; Bill Randles and myself were attacked in England by someone else in a discernment ministry, simply because we are not cessationists. Yes, arrogant men. There are some people who were very strongly influenced by Neo-Nazis in Australia; they are vehemently anti-Semitic and are constantly worsening. They are attacking Arnold Fruchtenbaum and myself, to name a few.

Even among the remnant, *look out!* The fact that someone realises the nature of deception does not necessarily mean they are one of us. They may be in our circle, but there are people in our circle who have their own agenda. We had a woman in our ministry in Pittsburgh; she thought I was wonderful because I spoke out against Toronto and all of that, yet I found out that she was secretly a Christian feminist who had been ordained by a heretic named Peter Michas, who denies the Trinity. She was an immoral woman who left her husband for another man from a discernment ministry in South Africa. Remember: *Satan wants to infiltrate the remnant.* The mainstream Judah was gone; he already had them. It was only the remnant who presented a problem for the king of Babylon. The same is true today; Satan isn't worried about what is going on inside First Assemblies of God – he has those people deceived already. Now he wants to get people into *your* church. And he'll do it.

Just because someone realises what's wrong, they are not automatically right. There are good people in the discernment movement, and there are also bad ones. In fact, I would say that there are as many bad ones as there are good ones. This is the world; they will attack anyone who truly tries to protect the sheep. They will attack the Jeremiahs, and they will attack the Baruchs. I've seen Dave Hunt attacked by people in discernment ministries; in fact, Dave Hunt is under attack right now by them. I have seen Bill Randles attacked, Philip Powell attacked, Jewel van der Merwe attacked, yours truly attacked, and by whom? By people outside of discernment circles? No – by people who are supposedly in discernment ministry. These people are quite arrogant.

Realise something: a good, faithful church will attract refugees from all the bad churches around it. Some of those people who come to your church will be utterly sincere; however, there are other people who, again, have an agenda. They are against any kind of authority unless it's their own, against any kind of commitment unless it's on their terms, and they will latch onto a good church simply because it becomes a platform for them, from which they wish to exercise their own interests. Once these good churches no longer accommodate what they want, they will turn against those churches. This happens everywhere; simply because someone is against what you are against does not guarantee that they are for what you are for. Real deception will increase in the Last Days. Just as they attacked Jeremiah and Baruch in the last days of Judah, so they are attacking Dave Hunt and Jewel van der Merwe today. It happened then, and it's happening now.

But let's look further, at Jeremiah 43:5-7:

> "But Johanan the son of Kareah and all the commanders of the forces took the entire remnant of Judah which had returned from the nations to which they had been driven away in order to reside in the land of Judah. The men, the women, the children, the king's daughters – every person whom Nebuzaradan the captain of the guard had left with Gedaliah the son of Ahikam the grandson of Shaphan, together with Jeremiah the prophet and Baruch the son of Neriah, and entered the land of Egypt. For they did not obey the voice of the LORD, and went as far as Tahpanhes."

Johanan seemed to be a good guy earlier. The deception in the last days becomes like intrigue. Early on, one of George Washington's best generals in fighting the American revolutionary war against the British was Benedict Arnold, who later became one of the British army's best generals against George Washington.

Jeremiah 43:8-10:

> "In Tahpanhes of Egypt, the word of the LORD came to Jeremiah: 'Take large stones in your hands and hide them in the mortar of the brick terrace which is at the entrance of Pharaoh's palace at Tahpanhes in the sight of some of the Jews, and say to them, 'Thus says the LORD God of Israel: Behold, I am going to send Nebuchadnezzar, the king of Babylon, My servant, and I am going to set his throne right over these stones that I have hidden, and he will spread his canopy over them.'"

Even Egypt came under the dominion of the king of Babylon. Look at Revelation 18:3, which says: *"For the nations have drunk of the wine of the passion of her immorality, and the kings of the earth have committed acts of immorality with her."* The kings of the earth; the merchants of the earth have become rich by the wealth of her sensuality. In the last days, the prosperity of the nations will depend on their relationship to Babylon. Revelation 13:11: *"The beast came up out of the earth and spoke, and he had two horns like a ram and like a dragon."* The earth is Israel; the other beast comes up out of the sea, which is the nations.

Jeremiah 44:30:

> "Thus says the LORD: 'Behold, I am going to give over Pharaoh Hophrah, king of Egypt, into the hand of his enemies, into the hand of those who seek his life, just as I gave over Zedekiah king of Judah into the hand of Nebuchadnezzar king of Babylon, who was his enemy and seeking his life.'"

If God gave the Hebrew king over to the king of Babylon, how much more quickly will He give the pagan king over? If the king of Babylon can get control of so much of the church, what is there to stop him from gaining control of the world? Nothing. It is a false security; a deadly false security.

But let us continue: Jeremiah 44:12-14:

> "I will take away the remnant of Judah that have set their minds on entering the land of Egypt to reside there, and they will all meet their end in the land of Egypt. They will fall by the sword and meet their end by famine; both small and great will die by the sword and famine, and become a curse, an object of horror, an imprecation and a reproach. And I will punish those who live in the land of Egypt just as I did those in Jerusalem, with the sword and with famine. So there will be no refugees or survivors for the remnant of Judah who have entered the land of Egypt to reside there, and then to return to the land of Judah to which they are longing to return to live. For none will return except a few refugees."

In the Bible, going to Egypt is always a picture of backsliding. When somebody backslides and goes into the world, the Holy Spirit convicts them and tries to bring them back. In the last days, however, it's different; very few of those who go into the world in the last days will make it back out. Going back to Egypt is dangerous at any time, but in the last days your chances of getting back to the Lord once you leave Him are very slim. How many people, for instance, are cured of aids? The odds are similar; very few will make it.

They had a choice: Babylon was death and Egypt was death; the only right choice was to stay in the palm of God.

Jeremiah 44:19 – this is going to be a big issue in the last days. I will tell you what the penultimate deception is going to be, the ultimate being the Antichrist. Do you notice in the book of Revelation that when the Antichrist is spoken of, there is always the figure of a woman in the background? She is the penultimate; he is the ultimate. And here is what it will be:

> "'And the women said, 'When we were burning sacrifices to the Queen of Heaven, and were pouring out libations to her, was it without our husbands that we made for her sacrificial cakes in her image and poured out libations to her?'"

Verse 24:

> Then Jeremiah said to all the people, including all the women, "Hear the word of the LORD, all Judah who are in the land of Egypt: thus says the Lord of hosts, the God of Israel – 'As for you and your wives, you have spoken with your mouths and fulfilled it with your hands, saying, 'We will certainly perform our vows that we have vowed to burn sacrifices to the Queen of Heaven, and pour out libations to her.' Go ahead and confirm your vows, and certainly perform your vows. Nevertheless hear the word of the LORD: All Judah who are living in the land of Egypt, behold, I have sworn by My great Name,' says the LORD, 'Never again shall My name be invoked by the mouth of any man of Judah in the land of Egypt, saying, 'As the LORD lives'. Behold, I am watching over them for harm, not for good, and all the men of Judah who are in the land of Egypt will meet their end by the sword and by famine until they are completely gone. And those who escape the sword will return out of the land of Egypt unto the land of Judah, once more few in number. Then all the remnant of Judah who have gone to the land of Egypt to reside there will know whose word will stand; theirs or Mine. And this will be the sign to you,' declares the LORD: 'I am going to punish you in this place so that you will know that My words will surely stand against you for harm.'"

The Queen of Heaven. The title of Pope John Paul II's book is *Totos Tuam Maria,* "All To You, Mary". He prays to Mary. The veneration of Mary is biblically a form of worship. The Catholic church doesn't call it worship, but something next to worship called 'hyperdulia'. What they don't know is this: the Hebrew word for idolatry is *avodah zarah* 'to serve'. By using the terms they use, they essentially admit that they are practicing idolatry, though they don't see it that way. However, if they knew what they were doing it would be – if a person bows down, that is an act of worship. They take it further, showering her with flowers and fancy garments, bowing down to her and singing *Ave Maria*. Mary worship will grow; she is the pseudo-Christianisation expressed culturally in many other cult deities.

Great is Diana of Ephesus – remember what happened at Ephesus in the book of Acts? Paul spoke against the worship of Diana and it caused a riot. When you warn against the veneration of Mary, you will get an angry and violent response. She is the current expression of the Queen of Heaven, to whom they will be sacrificing cakes. What began with Fatima and Lourdes, Medjugorje, Guadalupe – all over the world – will continue to grow. Mount Carmel, in Israel, has been the site of many supposed apparitions of Mary. It also happens to be the very same place where Ashtaroth, a female goddess, was worshipped in the Bible.

Catholics are going to get more and more into it, and you will find Protestants going along with it. Already we have evangelical bishops marching in Walsingham, England, in a procession to Mary. This will continue to grow worse.

God says, "I will not give My glory to another." God says, "There is one intercessor between God and man, Jesus the Righteous." Their worship of Mary contradicts these things, among others. Understand that the thing they call Mary is not truly Mary; they only think it is she. Similarly, the Mormons call themselves the Church of Jesus Christ of Latter-Day Saints – but their Jesus Christ is not the one of the Bible. Their Jesus is the half- brother of Satan. The Mary of the Catholic church is not the Mary of scripture. I'm not speaking against the real Mary – she was the greatest woman who ever lived. She was the mother of the Messiah; but she herself proclaimed her own need of a saviour in the Magnificat, in Luke 2:47: *'My. . . spirit rejoices in God my Saviour'*. Just as in denouncing the Mormon 'Jesus' I am not denouncing the real Jesus, so in denouncing the Catholic Mary I am not denouncing the real Mary. What they have comes straight from Babylon – the pagan Queen of Heaven. As the Mary-worship grows, you will find evangelical Protestants going along with it in increasing numbers; that will be the next trend.

How does this end? You have Egypt, you have Babylon, or you have the palm of God. The obvious is, don't go to Babylon, and don't think you can make peace with it. Don't go to Egypt, because if you do your chances of getting back are very slim. Don't think you can preserve your faith in the world; it won't work, just as the men from Judah who resided in Egypt could no longer call on the name of the Lord. Both ways end in death.

Expect people in discernment ministries to display arrogance; they will attack their own brethren in those circles in the way that Baruch and Jeremiah were attacked in their time. You will find people who had been leaders against the deception, just as Johanan was, turning against others in the circle. Why? Because they are going into the world. Expect it to happen.

Expect the veneration of Mary to begin growing very much larger; not only among the Catholics and the Greek Orthodox, but even among so- called Protestants; even evangelical Protestants. Already we have Charismatic Catholics who pray in tongues to Mary. Expect this to happen.

But what's the bottom line in all of this? What about those of us who want to stay in Geruth Kimham, who are longing for Jesus to come back? What does God say to those who will not go to Egypt, who will not go to Babylon, and who will not burn incense to the Queen of Heaven?

> "If you will indeed stay in this land, I will build you up and not tear you down. I will plant you and not uproot you."

Finally, God tells Jeremiah this in chapter 45:5:

> "But you, are you seeking great things for yourself? Do not seek them, for behold, I am going to bring disaster on all flesh," declares the LORD. "But I will give your life to you as booty in all the places where you may go."

Don't expect much out of this place. I've always tried to raise my children with the following philosophy: plan *for* the future, but don't plan *on* it.

Don't seek great things for yourself. If God gives you a great ministry, praise the Lord! But don't seek that – seek to survive.

If God gives you some material success, don't let it go to your head

– use it for God's glory, but don't seek it and don't pursue it. Pursue survival.

How quickly can a stock market crash? How quickly can the Middle East explode into a thermonuclear holocaust? How quickly can a handful of Islamic terrorists with biological weapons wipe out half of Sydney, or New York, thinking of it as *jihad*?

No, my friends, we will have our lives as our booty. *"If you will indeed stay in this land, then I will build you up,"* says God. *"Don't be afraid of the king of Babylon, for I am with you to save you and to deliver you from his hand."*

That is His promise.

Other books by Jacob Prasch:

Final Words of Jesus & Satan's Lies Today
ISBN 19015460 6 3

Grain for the Famine
ISBN 19015460 8 X

Raising the Axe head
19015460 7 1

(co-authored with Siam Bhayro, Philip Foster, Tony Pearce and Philip Powell)

Available from:

SMP Ltd
24 Geldart Street
Cambridge CB1 2LX UK
tel + (0)1223 504871
fax + (0)1223 512304
Email: PF.SMP@dial.pipex.com